Praise for of
THEODORE TAYLOR

The Cay: Mr. Taylor has provided an exciting story . . . The idea that all humanity would benefit from this special form of color blindness permeates the whole book . . . The result is a story with a high ethical purpose but no sermon. *The New York Times*

A taut, tightly compressed story of endurance and revelation . . . at once barbed and tender, tense and fragile—as Timothy would say, "Outrageous good." *Kirkus Reviews, starred*

Fully realized setting . . . artful unobtrusive use of dialect . . . the representation of a hauntingly deep love, the poignancy of which is rarely achieved. *School Library Journal, starred*

༚

The Maldonado Miracle: A fast moving and convincing story with all the richness of characterization and detail that are hallmarks of Theodore Taylor's fiction. *Booklist*

(A *Showtime* film directed by Salma Hayek, October 2003.)

༚

Teetoncey: Taylor has us walking the beaches, smelling the salt air and watching the sky for storm signals. *The New York Times*

(First of the Cape Hatteras trilogy to be re-published by Harcourt.)

༚

Walking Up a Rainbow: Taylor has crafted a tale that is such a page-turner that it is hard to imagine any junior high schooler who wouldn't come along for the ride. *Book Report*

∽○∽

The Hostage: Superior writing makes *The Hostage* a joy to read. *Christian Science Monitor*

∽○∽

Sniper: With trapping perfect for the edge of a chair, Taylor's latest novel makes gripping reading. *Booklist*

∽○∽

The Trouble with Tuck: Leaves the reader with a warm glow. It is a story of devotion between a dog and his mistress and the testing of that love when the dog goes blind. *St. Louis Post-Dispatch*

∽○∽

The Bomb: A haunting personal and soundly researched work about the testing of an atom bomb post–World War II at Bikini Atoll. *Publisher's Weekly*

Writing simply but powerfully, Taylor has passed his memories on to generations who may only associate Bikini Atoll to swimsuits. *Booklist*

∽○∽

A Sailor Returns: A wonderful book for anyone who has a special relationship with a grandparent or longs for one. *School Library Journal*

∽○∽

The Boy Who Could Fly Without a Motor: Taylor's tight writing and flair for the fanciful keeps this caper airborne. *Publisher's Weekly*

∽○∽

To Kill The Leopard: A high impact techno-thriller. Theodore Taylor's first adult novel is a winner. *Publisher's Weekly*

～o～

The Weirdo: This murder mystery/love story/environmental thriller weaves an uncommon spell. *Publisher's Weekly*

(Winner of a 1992 Mystery Writers of America "Edgar.")

～o～

Rogue Wave and Other Red-Blooded Sea Stories: Juicy subjects such as sharks, a cruel captain and a psychological battle between a captured Nazi U-boat commander and a scholarly British intelligence officer are fleshed out in a very masculine way. *Booklist*

～o～

Maria: This beautiful story will leave readers warm, satisfied and gently reminded of the real meaning of Christmas. *Booklist*

～o～

Lord of the Kill: *Sequel to Sniper.* When the body of a young Asian woman is found mauled to death in the jaguar compound, Taylor masterfully creates an accessible mystery while weaving together fascinating information about big cats. *School Library Journal*

～o～

Sweet Friday Island: It is refreshing to read a novel that features a female teenager with a close and positive relationship with her divorced father. *American Booksellers*

Making Love to
TYPEWRITERS

Making Love to
TYPEWRITERS

THEODORE TAYLOR

Ivy House
Publishing Group
www.ivyhousebooks.com

PUBLISHED BY IVY HOUSE PUBLISHING GROUP
5122 Bur Oak Circle, Raleigh, NC 27612
United States of America
919-782-0281
www.ivyhousebooks.com

ISBN: 1-57197-429-6
Library of Congress Control Number: 2004105754

Printed in the United States of America

For my Tar Heel nephew Donald Beam,
of Marion, North Carolina

Prologue

I think that my first awareness of being on earth in North Carolina came when I was about four. The night was cold and unrelieved by stars, the moon was down. I was on my father's shoulder; my mother and older sister, Mary, were by his side. We were spectators on the hard scrabble roadside, totally silent, one of those times when words do not add a blessed thing to sight and sound. In 1925, we lived on the outskirts of Statesville, a cotton mill town.

Slowly coming up the dirt road were a round dozen Ku Klux Klanners, holding pineknot torches, their flour-white robes immaculate and starched, the red flames reflecting down upon them. Their big horses were snuffling, vapor puffing from their nostrils. The faceless men looked over at us through their slits, eyes boring. Thinking about it much later, I believe they were trying to say, "We're here to save you, to save the white race . . ."

Back inside the house, I'm sure my mother and Mary later explained to me what the Klanners were all about, hoping that a four-year-old mind would grasp the group's intent. I presume that it did for the simple reason that the scene on that country road has rewound and replayed in my mind many times, even down to the harsh breathing and muffled clip-clops of the horses. Any time there has been a printed or TV mention of the hooded men, I have a flashback.

Now and then, over the years, I'd remind my mother of that terrifying night and ask about it again, making absolutely certain it was not a dream. "Where were they going? What were they going to do?"

They might plant Christ's cross in an uppity black farmer's yard, Mother said. Or they might burn his shanty, she said.

Statesville had its share of racism. "Nigger" was much more acceptable than "Negro" or "Culluud" or black. I heard the words many times in my childhood but no one in our family except my father ever used them. My mother reacted immediately whenever she heard them. A brave, deeply religious woman of German heritage, she would say sternly, "Don't use that word in my presence." There was reaction, of course, from those reprimanded. Some bristled; some were ashamed. My father would only laugh and shrug.

Several years ago I looked but found no record of any black person ever being strung from a tree in the Statesville area. We weren't in the Deep South and were spared at least that final Klan act. The image of the KKK riders stayed with me. In 1968, when I began writing *The Cay*, an adventure novel with racial overtones, I recalled vividly those hard eyes, those snuffling horses, and the torches that cast their angry red glow over the road.

Located in the heart of the Piedmont area of North Carolina, on the red-earth flatlands before the western rises of the Blue Ridges, Statesville had about ten thousand inhabitants when I was born in summer, 1921. County seat of Iredell, my hometown was defined by its agriculture economy—cotton, tobacco, corn; fruit orchards; truck farms. Near the old railway station was a brickyard and the foundry, where my often belligerent father worked for a while after being fired from a Greensboro plant. That was his Irish problem—always getting fired.

Knitting mills provided most of the jobs. It was a sleepy, God-fearing, Waspish town of the upper South, related in some ways to novelist Thomas Wolfe's town of "Altamont," in Asheville, up in the Blue Ridges. Some of the people of his *Look Homeward, Angel*, as I remember them, could probably have been found in Statesville. It was the chewing tobacco capital of the world—fifty-five different brands—and, for a while, the legitimate corn liquor capital of the world. Prohibition dealt it a terrible blow and dozens of "white lightning" moonshine stills soon spread around the county, bringing in dozens of federal revenue agents, the "Revenoors." Exciting shotgun times, I recall.

It was still rebel land. There was a large statue of a Confederate soldier on the courthouse lawn, along with a cannon and two stacks of cannonballs. Local Iredell rebel Captain Absolem Simonton was celebrated. I can still hear faintly, "Look away, look away, look away, Dixieland." A "Damn Yankee" was a person, a "come-here" who came to Statesville and stayed. A "plain Yankee" was a visitor from the north who fortunately returned to Yankeeland. Good riddance, our people said. In many ways, I'm still a rebel, I admit.

Never in my childhood did I want to become a writer. Early on, I had a thing for trees—tall, leafy ones. I climbed the highest ones I could find. My father once asked, "Do you plan to become a monkey?" That would have been fine, swinging from limb to limb. Or perhaps become an explorer? I sought out drainpipes to investigate and once got stuck in one.

I often walked the fields and forests alone, roaming free as a squirrel. Spring, summer, autumn, and winter, with no particular destination or mission. I did this when I was seven, eight, or nine, so long ago; listening to the birds, other sounds of the woods, celebrating being alone.

With three or four other boys I played Huck Finn and rafted down the Catawba when I was no more than nine. My mother never asked, "Where are you going?" Off to explore, of course. She trusted God that I'd come safely home. Several times I came close to joining Him. With another kid, a black kid, I once crossed an abandoned wooden bridge that had been built during the Civil War. The earth was a hundred feet below and rotten pieces of wood kept falling away beneath our feet. Exploration! A writer needs to explore, mentally and physically.

But the land was gentle, as were most of the people living in it. Mother said she thought it was fine when I told her I'd gotten a paper route. I was up at four in the morning to walk to the Vance Hotel and wait for the Greyhound driver to toss off the *Greensboro Daily News*. Walking through the still darkness at age nine, not once did I think of harm. Then off to school I trudged in knickers and a cap. I doubt many current moms would allow such predawn work for their nine-year-olds.

I look back on a lifetime at the typewriter, many typewriters in many places, and marvel at how lucky I've been. On those keys I have pecked out sports and crime and love and death. I've two-fin-gered books for adults and young readers, as well as scripts for radio, TV, and feature films. I've been so very, very lucky. Here I am still learning the three C's of good storytelling: character, conflict, and construction. And I'm still pecking away.

GROWING UP

Cherished Statesville days: Playing marbles in rings drawn on brick-hard clay; climbing the tall Mitchell College water tower to see around the world, imagining England over there, China down there; skinny dipping in creeks the color of light mud; riding in old Model T Fords; smoking dry coffee grains, dried corn silk, and dried monkey tree pods before age ten, then moving on to Lucky Strikes and Chesterfields, or the butts of any brand picked up from the street, never thinking about what deadly germs the last mouth possessed; coming out of the movie house and sitting down in a grassy hole about a block away to contemplate the marvelous *picture show.* I was totally unaware I was training to be a writer. I suppose I was just honing imagination.

There was a World War I picture show, now a classic, entitled *All Quiet on the Western Front* that I attended with a few neighborhood boys. Then we came home and dug trenches. We made rifles out of tongue-and-groove boards, using the grooves to fire arrows with cut-out strips of auto inner tubes as the propellants. We shot at each other, unconcerned that we might put an eye out. We re-enacted other picture shows, cowboy shows in particular.

I made cars out of junked wagon wheels, with boards for the

bodies, steering them with a rope attached to the front axles. They flew down the few hilly roads. My world at the time was far away from the world in which girls lived.

Cherished nights: Going to the Statesville farmer's market on Saturday nights at age five or six, their Conestoga-type wagons illuminated with pineknot torches; fishing for catfish on Catawba River shores, hoping the snakes wouldn't crawl out to the lantern light; playing hide-and-seek in graveyards; treasure hunts all over town, including the graveyards.

The times when my father was home, not very often, he'd take me hunting or fishing, depending on the season. At the time, I looked forward to an existence in the hunting fields as an adult or on lakes or rivers, out on the seas. He once told me he should have been a sports guide instead of an ironworker. Then he wouldn't have bosses. That sounded good to me. I'd become a hunting and fishing guide as an adult.

I'm told that my father bought me a bamboo fishing pole when I was three, and I remember clearly the 410 gauge shotgun that he bought for my tenth birthday. I used it to shoot rabbits among the winter cornstalks. I wouldn't think of owning a shotgun now nor of shooting a rabbit. I'm an animal rights person.

∾◦∾

Dr. Thomas Anderson, our new landlord, was a superb Southern storyteller. A lonely widower, he befriended me not long after the Klan incident. We'd just moved into town. Our friendship lasted until my family moved away to Virginia.

The last public hanging in Statesville took place in the summer of 1905, the victim a poor white farmer falsely convicted of first degree murder. A crowd estimated at 1,000 surrounded the courthouse to witness the event. Dr. Anderson was there. The accused had a black hood over his head, and the other participants on the gallows platform wore black, including a deputy sheriff with a white rose in his lapel. I have a newspaper photo of the scene at the gallows. The farmer's wife took her husband's body home in a wagon drawn by a pair of black mules, two small children sitting beside her.

Dr. Anderson told me about it in great detail when I was about eleven. Dr. Anderson, as part-time coroner, made the official death announcement. Eventually, I wrote a short story involving the "last hanging sheriff" of Iredell County and the young widow who buried her husband, having dug his grave herself. In my unpublished story sent to a half-dozen magazines, the deputy sheriff and the widow fall in love. Deserved story rejections have been a part of my life ever since.

Dr. Anderson, already in his seventies, lived in a truly grand house about forty feet away from us. We rented a much lesser house from him for twenty dollars a month. He was my companion on many occasions; his own children were grown and away. In his early days he'd ridden horses to reach his patients, covering as many as fifteen miles in the dead of winter. I remember his brown hat and white brush of mustache and high white collar, his pocket watch and long gold chain. Sometimes I slept in his horsebarn loft, liking the smell of his mare. Dr. Anderson had been ten years old when the Civil War began, and he recalled Confederate troops marching by. Some were teenagers, he said, no more than fourteen or fifteen years old.

He took me to Ringling Brothers, Barnum and Bailey, or whatever circuses came to town, and we'd watch as they unloaded the dawn trains, elephants helping; before we took in the matinee performance. The elephants were used like mules to drag equipment. He took me to carnivals, buying peanuts and cotton candy, exposing me to freak shows and chance games. I stored up, as writers should. Dr. Anderson often served as my surrogate father, with skinny-kid me wondering where my real father was and what he was doing.

A small man with twinkling eyes, I now realize the doctor had a macabre sense of humor. I was maybe eight the day he pointed out "The Hanging Tree" from which Tom Dula had been stretched in

1868 for the famed murder of Laura Foster at Deep Gap, not too far away. Others maintained that Tom had been stretched from a regular gallows in that Statesville field. I went back later, by myself, to take another look at that tree. A writer should re-check the scene.

The Kingston Trio immortalized Tom Dula with a folk ballad in the late fifties: "Hang Down Your Head, Tom Dooley . . . " I gathered research for a Tom Dula story long ago but have yet to write it, one of many aging research packets untouched for my writing daughter Wendy to inherit. A case can be made for chivalrous Tom taking the rap for Annie Melton, a rival of Laura Foster for Tom's love. More than 150 years later I think Annie was the one who killed Laura, not Tom. Dr. Anderson believed that to be true.

According to the *Statesville Record,* an old, old grandmother stood by Annie's deathbed and heard sounds like "red hot rocks being dropped in a bucket of cold water." Annie Melton herself claimed she could see "flames of hell at the foot of her bed." She was indeed guilty and poor Tom took the rope. How delicious! That story has the heady stuff of love and murder. I heard some other mighty good stories as a child, all in the tradition of Southern storytelling. They shaped me.

Some of the Statesville events and characters have stayed with me. Essential colors, sounds, smells, characters. They were pieces of the town's fabric when I was growing up. I'm sure there are forgotten others, undoubtedly stored in my subconscious, there to stay. I have two filing cabinets full of yellowing notes and research.

I remember one Sunday night when I was six or seven, I was walking from the train station with my father on the town's busiest street when a Model T Ford, billowing gray-white smoke, sped by us, chased by cops in an open Chicago-style black touring car. The straw-hatted farmer/corn liquor bootlegger at the wheel had kerosene dripping on the car's hot exhaust pipe, causing the smoke. I was hoping he'd get away, rooting for the underdog even then. I later used the scene in a short story that never sold. My father was in and out of my life like the bootlegger dodging the cops.

I also recall Saturday morning rituals at the courthouse when bootleggers' product, confiscated the previous week, was dumped into the gutter, the strong smell lingering for hours. Jokesters said that all the Statesville Creek frogs had hangovers on Sundays. I could have been the curious boy on a Norman Rockwell *Saturday Evening Post* cover, a spectator in tweed knee-pants, sniffing the air. I was just a crooked-toothed boy with a memory bank storing yet another scent.

At one time, there were three madstones in the Iredell County area that were used to treat hydrophobia, or mad dog bites. Hydrophobia killed after agonizing pain. A madstone was a small brown rock, a little larger than a partridge egg. A rental, it was applied to a dog or snake bite. This was before the Pasteur treatment. After one terrible dog attack, two local men reportedly got into an argument over ownership of one of the madstones and sawed it in half. A rabid dog, a little girl dying, and two rednecks quarreling with a saw! A short story? I thought so years afterward. My 1947 story never sold.

At one time, post-Revolutionary War, there was a state law involving perjury, plain old lying under oath. "The penalty was having both ears sliced off," Dr. Anderson said with a chuckle. Shorn ears were nailed to the town's outdoor pillory until sundown. Then they were fed to dogs. It is a shame that we don't have that law for today's Washington politicians. Imagine Bill Clinton without his ears. There was a famous case in the Statesville court that ended the practice because of undue harshness. "There were men, and women, around the state with no ears," Dr. Anderson said. Fine courtroom drama waiting to be written.

Childhood memory is so hit and miss. Mine is, anyway. There seem to be layers triggered by a few words, unpeeling when least expected. Or a glimpse, maybe a larger sight, jogs something deep within my brain. Then there's the tricky part when a forgotten name or incident is flushed out unexpectedly by the unconscious. At least, that's the way it works for me in a profession often dependent on memory.

I suspect that I first thought about writing books after my sister Mary introduced me to Steinbeck and Hemingway, in that order. Not once did she say, "That's too old for you." She said, "You must read them." I was ten or eleven then. My mother frowned. What was Mary thinking about?

I'm told I was very shy as a small child, the kind that clung to mother's skirt. And in certain situations I remain shy to this day, preferring to circulate among people I know well, developing new friendships slowly, perfectly happy to write each day in a room surrounded by trees, with a dog asleep in the corner or under the desk and Andrea Bocelli singing softly. I have workday contact with cats and birds, seldom humans. There are huge glass windows on three sides, gardens and greenery all around, the Pacific Ocean within earshot when the surf pounds.

The first stories of my childhood were mainly the bible adventures, loaded with action. David slaying Goliath; Samson and Delilah; Samson pulling down the Philistine temple. Mother read them to me countless times when I was three or four. I'm now certain she'd had it with Samson but she never complained.

There were four daughters and a son born to Edward Riley Taylor and Elnora Alma Langhans before I came along. That son, Edward, had died three years previously at the age of three. I suppose we were an ordinary family. My father, first of all, though of absolute English descent, swore he was an Irishman, and certainly had that temperament, though a teetotaler. At times, he called himself "Riley." Argumentative, I dread to think how he might have been as a saloon regular. A singer of Irish songs, he would have brawled with many a Houlihan or Kelly or O'Brien with roundhouse rights. Rebellious, the typical "black sheep," he never finished grade school and went to work in a Pittsburgh foundry as an apprentice iron molder, the ne'er-do-well of a well-to-do family. His father was a respected Westinghouse company executive and his college graduate brothers were also successful businessmen. To my knowledge, and to the knowledge of my sisters and mother, he never once contacted his family after leaving home. When his father died, a brother wired him. My father said, at the dinner table, showing no emotion, "Dad died yesterday." Then he sat in his bedroom rocking chair all night. He did not respond to the funeral notification. I wish I'd known what his thoughts were. I wish I'd known who he was.

I loved my father in my early years. Later, as a teenager, there were times I literally hated him. Ashamedly now, I recall being forced to massage his heavy back muscles with rubbing alcohol or shave the back of his neck or type his labor propaganda letters. Petty things, I know, but I fumed. In my teens, I could look back and understand the dark hatred of two of my sisters: He had failed to provide for our mother, to give her the things in life she so richly deserved; and he failed to provide for my sisters and me. He was monumentally self-ish, possessed by left-wing politics. I've never written about him until now. I do so now with pain.

I have a foggy memory of a boxy little white clapboard house, my first house. After the clapboard, the Ku Klux Klan ride-by house, we lived in another five houses within ten years, always moving without explanation, always living in "workingman" houses. My father; oh, my father.

There were periods, especially during the Depression of the late 1920s and early 1930s, when I would not see him for months—nothing new to the Taylor girls. He was a blue-collar workingman's workingman and earlier had become involved in the International Workers of the World, the "Wobblies," a left-wing labor organiza-tion. He was an organizer. In truth, he was a Communist sympa-thizer. When I was only four or five I remember him coming home one night bloodied and bruised, the result of tangling with police during a strike. At least once, police came to our house and took him away.

I remember walking beside him in a Memorial Day parade when I was five or six. He was a veteran of the Spanish-American

War, an Army private, and pointed out the ancient Confederate Veterans plodding along beside us to the band music, some proudly wearing parts of their old uniforms. The old men were mostly ram-rod straight, their lined faces filled with memories of the terrible battles between North and South. My father walked proudly.

There was an old grist mill not too far from Statesville, up a dirt road, with a huge wooden wheel that had powered the 1800s corn grinder which turned from the rushing crystal clear creek water. It was a place of quiet enchantment. We sat silently side-by-side on White's mill pond bank to catch catfish and crappie. He never talked much to me, then or later.

Later, I remember going with him to Lake Drummond, in the Dismal Swamp on the border of North Carolina and Virginia, the outboard pushing the borrowed fifteen-foot wooden boat up the Feeder Ditch. Sunning snakes hung from the thick branches above, sometimes falling into the boat. He'd flip them out without comment. I was always afraid of the Dismal, and it eventually became site of my novel *The Weirdo*, 1991. I am still afraid of snakes. My second wife Flora and I almost walked into a patch of cobras in Sri Lanka on a round-the-world research trip. Retreat was a good idea.

I try to remember the good things about my father. He didn't physically abuse my sisters nor my mother nor me, aside from once locking me in a closet. But studied neglect is another form of abuse.

He was home for one Christmas in my early life, a German Christmas, of course: candle-lit tree not seen until Christmas morning, magically appearing in the living room. There were noises on the roof. "Reindeer," Mother said.

It was several years before I realized it had been my father up there.

∞∞∞

My mother was so different from my father that we children could not understand how these two people got together and married. She, fragile and delicate; he, rough and muscular. Mother, reciting poetry; father, talking about the "workingman" endlessly. His consuming enemies were bosses, bankers, corporation heads, and Republicans. Her heroes were men of God, poets, and writers. The German influence of her childhood was strong. Her blood was from Holstein. She spoke the language. She was so gentle and creative; he was so ungentle and uncreative. She wanted to be an actress. Now, she was a mother, seamstress and cook. She used a foot-pedal Singer.

Sometimes she'd stop in the middle of making a pie and dramatically throw an arm into the air in a final curtain flourish, shouting, "Excelsior, excelsior!" Onward, upward!

I wondered sometimes what her life might have been like if she'd married someone who saw worth and value and joy in the stage, music, poetry, and fine art. They were wed in August, 1900, in Avalon, Pennsylvania. I'm told that her father, brothers, and a sister were shocked by her choice of a mate. Finally I discovered, through my sisters, that the marriage was to escape a mean-spirited step-mother, a living witch. Now and then I've thought about a novel based on the marriage. I don't have the heart to do it. Grown, my sisters finally urged her to divorce him but there'd never been a divorce in the Langhans family and she foolishly refused to break the marriage vows. What price pride? That became my problem later on, refusing to file during a broken marriage.

My father moved my mother several times in the Pittsburgh area after being fired from jobs and then took his family to Toronto. Another foundry job. Soon a Canadian doctor advised him to take my mother south because of poor health. He chose North Carolina but no one remembers why.

In the farmhouse on the outskirts of Greensboro, my mother, with her long fingers, did candlelight shadow figures on the wall for the young sisters, making up stories to go with them. Perhaps my love affair with words goes back to before I was born, if that is possible.

The Taylors were house-sitting free for an absentee owner. One night, this same farmhouse, with all the females inside, received a shotgun blast in response to my father's earlier quarrel with a neighbor. My father, unfortunately, wasn't home. He'd gone who-knew-where. When he returned for a visit and was told of the incident, he shrugged.

Naoma was first born, then along came Eleanor, Louise, and Mary, none of them alike in looks or personality. Mother named them from the bible. The North Carolina stories of the Taylor Girls are still being recorded on tape, filling in the gaps before I was born in case I do novelize them. In the house near the cold and windy French Broad River in Asheville, they searched the basement for coal left over from the last tenant. Sometimes they put blankets over their shoulders when eating supper. Mother didn't let them cook for fear of wasting food.

Mother set a high standard for her young daughters as well as herself in the small towns, determined that they wouldn't drawl, that they wouldn't become Southern women, and that they wouldn't marry Southern men. She was strict with them, raising them in the Lutheran church, and for one who appeared so fragile and tubercular, she had a steely inner strength that seldom bent. It was a side of her that I worshiped.

While my father was *who-knows-where*, Mother read Dickens and Shakespeare and *Jane Eyre* to the girls in the evenings. She read stories of fairies, goblins, and elves to them. She showed them how to build fairy houses of leaves and twigs and grasses. Sometimes, on hot summer evenings in Franklin village, after the dew fell and the fireflies came out, the Taylor Girls could be seen dancing on the lawn in their white nightgowns. I wish I'd been there.

I come from a family of determined women and was influenced by them. Naoma was the first to leave home. In her late teens, she married a minister in New York. He became mentally ill and chased her with a butcher knife. Eventually, he was committed to an insane asylum and spent the rest of his life there. Then she married a New York bank executive. Also story material, I think.

As a teenager Eleanor lied about her age and experience to get a teaching certificate. She always took pride in her ability to accomplish whatever she set out to do. I tried to follow her. She and Louise began teaching grade school students in Coolemee and Catfish villages as teens, while Louise lived with a mountain bootlegger family—another source of stories. They led the way for my own teenage experiences. *Never fear leaving home.* Pack up and go! I did.

Eleanor left North Carolina at eighteen and worked at various jobs in Manhattan. She married a Britisher and lived in London for a while. So from England came lead soldiers and fat children's books for my shelf with a different look and feel, a combination of text with richly drawn illustration, featuring English characters. *The Pip and Squeak Annuals* and the *Bo Peep Bumper Books* were my favorites, circa 1925. I still have them.

The youngest of the sisters, Mary, tall and slim with a model's bone structure, ten years older than I, became the last of the four at home while I was growing up. She daringly smoked in public, something that "ladies" weren't supposed to do in Statesville at the time. I even remember her brand, Raleighs. I'd sneak one or two now and then. She was a combined big sister/brother. I'll never know how she got her sophistication in that small Southern town.

I guess I'm a combination of my mother and my sisters. After my mother, it was Mary who influenced me the most. She always set an example by talking to me as though I were an adult; by the books she read and put on my nightstand; by craving to leave Statesville whenever my father decided to become financially responsible for my mother and myself, if ever. He finally did, twelve years after I was born.

I was the benefactor of all this female upgrowth. I heard some original elfin and goblin stories and saw the shadow fingers when of knee-pants age. I was also the benefactor of my brother's death, a strange way of putting it, I suppose. My mother had wanted a boy so badly after all her girls. Three-year-old Edward had what was thought to be a bad cold and was running a high fever on a winter's morning in 1919 when Louise and Mary went off to school. When they returned that afternoon he was dead of lobar pneumonia. It was devastating to my mother and sisters. Mother never really recovered from his death and changed dramatically, now viewing life as something entirely fleeting. In turn, I took Edward's place. She'd been Germanically stern with my sisters but seldom said no to me.

Sunday school each and every Sunday, then to church service, then to vespers; then to Wednesday night prayer meeting, summer church school, Bible study. I was getting wacky from the Jesus connection. My father, who was Roman Catholic, did not attend any church. Occasionally, my mother would take me to the Center Street African Methodist Episcopal Zion Church so that we could listen to the spirituals. We were always welcome.

I've tackled racial prejudice in several books but my only black playmate of childhood was Luke, son of our washerwoman, Matilda. Since my father was continually broke, my mother's brothers sent much-needed checks and one of her few luxuries was to have the laundry done in a huge iron kettle in the backyard, over a wood fire. Matilda would bring Luke along two Saturdays each month and we'd play one game or another or just prowl around the woods. I don't remember any other contact with black children. It just wasn't done in Statesville.

The only truly spooky building in Statesville was the Wallace Herbarium, at the foot of Walnut, my street. It was an unpainted, age-blackened wooden structure, three stories high, with a cupola at top, built before the Civil War. Norman Rockwell would have whipped out his brushes at the sight. It was owned by the Wallaces, Isaac and Lewis Elias, who had arrived from Germany to go into the medicinal herb business. They'd heard the countryside around Statesville was abundant with sassafras root and bark, wild cherry bark, penny royal leaves, catnip, sarsaparilla, and especially ginseng, prized by the Chinese. The smells coming from that building were strange and heady. With only plants in there, no lights were ever seen at night. I was told ghosts lived in that remarkable building; I believed that was true. I wish I could find a writing place for it, just for the sinister looks.

Next door was a tiny tin-roofed house, with a crooked tin pipe stack, residence of the caretaker, another Norman Rockwell possibility. He was tall and thin, always dressed in black like a funeral attendant. I was frightened of him, though he gave me no reason. But I ran if I happened to see him. He was surely out of Edgar Alan Poe, with his big black hat and bony frame. Or perhaps that's what the eyes of a child saw. While in the movie business later on I thought of that herbarium as a set for a spine-tingler, a juicy place for murder.

Prowl is such a wonderful word, animal-like in a sense, a sleek jaguar hunting in the jungle. I prowled constantly, a curious boy unknowingly in training to be an architect of words. The Statesville area was crisscrossed with creeks and I visited most of them. Second Creek, Third Creek, Fourth Creek, Fifth Creek, Beaver, Cooper. No one seemed to know why there wasn't a First Creek. The Catawba and South Yadkin Rivers were nearby. I hitchhiked with a fishing pole and worms when I was seven or eight to the banks of the Yadkin, never once thinking of harm. Never. A barefoot, straw-hatted boy by the road, thumb up. Who's to harm? I rode farmers' Model T trucks and horse-drawn wagons.

I roamed interesting places in and around town solo, hanging out at the blacksmith shop down from Center Street, watching horses being shod; the abandoned headquarters barn of our volunteer state cavalry, where *Dammit* and *Douglas,* two big geldings, charge-leaders, were celebrated; the old brickyard; the vacant strong-smelling building where chewing tobacco had once been manufactured. I crawled in numerous drainpipes (I got stuck in one, a sequence in *Tuck Triumphant,* 1991) and other places of mystery, such as abandoned farmhouses. I was collecting the stuff of stories, without the slightest knowledge I'd ever write fact or fiction.

I think I was about seven when I began to play with a boy named Phillip who lived not far away from Walnut and Oak. I thought he was a nice boy in all ways except one: His mother had taught him that all "Negroes" were "dumb and smelled." She said, "That's why they'd been slaves." Phillip believed it, of course.

My mother said, "You've been to their church. You know how they are, dressed so well on Sundays, always so warm and polite. They aren't dumb. Phillip's mother is wicked." It was the first time I'd ever heard her talk negatively about anyone. Years later he became the "Phe-leep" Enright of *The Cay*, 1969.

∽•∾

I soon acquired another surrogate father. The next-to-youngest sister, Louise, had married another teacher, Hugh Beam, a North Carolinian to my mother's exasperation. He was six-feet-four and weighed about 290. Ex-football tackle, he was a merry, cigar-smoking farmer's son who occasionally wrestled a black bear at a filling station, cracked pork bones with his teeth, and did other feats of strength that held me in awe. He'd throw me high in the air, maybe ten feet, then catch me. He bought fireworks for me on the Fourth of July and Christmas.

I spent some of the happiest days of my childhood in company with the huge man from Lincolnton. After coaching winning football, he finally went into politics and served in the state assembly, then became a lawyer and judge. Hugh Beam turned me into a rabid football fan and I remain one to this day. I watch college games on Saturdays, pro games on Sundays, and never miss a Monday night snap. A wonderful TV Saturday is football 9 A.M. to 10 P.M., to Flora's vexation. I hope that when I get to heaven, where I might go, there will be a channel to watch football.

My elementary school years, money was a big problem for millions of people, the depths of the Depression, after the stock market crash, and I went about trying to solve our money woes in my own way. I began raising greens behind our rented house to sell to markets, Mother helping to till the rich soil. I sold candy bars by the box, buying them wholesale, going door-to-door. I picked up scrap metal and hauled it in a wagon to Gordon's junkyard. I sold the *Saturday Evening Post* for a nickel, profiting two cents. I'm not the least sorry that I went through the scarcity of nickels and dimes. My mother would have taken the rack rather than go on welfare, which didn't exist, anyway. We never missed a meal though some nights we had fried apples for supper. They were picked from the tree next door, with permission.

Mary was earning fifteen a week at the local Chevrolet agency as a bookkeeper. Without Mary and my Pittsburgh uncles supporting us, the Statesville days would have been disastrous. I know I learned work ethics and the satisfaction of self-support, the uselessness of envy. Playing now and then with a rich kid, son of a chewing tobacco and snuff mogul, I did envy his Lionel train and small Elgin bike but I knew he wasn't a bit happier than I was.

My personal library card for the Statesville Public Library came along about the age of eight. By the time we moved to Johnson City, Tennessee, I was bringing home books that made my mother cringe, good church lady that she was, yet there was no censorship. In addition to all the Tom Swifts and Horatio Algers and Huck Finns and L. Frank Baums, I remember lugging in adult mysteries and detective stories.

We spent a year in Johnson City, when I was ten and money had all but vanished. My father learned that he could stay well fed in the Veteran's Hospital by claiming an injury. Mary supplied the boardinghouse money for mother and myself and I continued adventuring. I climbed a mountain for the view after I heard there was a great spring halfway up, and I spent time around a locomotive yard where old engines were parked, imagining I was an engineer. Once I stole a dime from my mother's purse to see a horror movie, and a huge cooking gas tank blew up while I was walking home in the dark, turning the sky red for miles around. I was being punished, I thought, and never again stole even a penny from her.

My father punched a fellow "patient" at the hospital and was kicked out. We didn't see him for almost a year, having no idea where he was. We'd moved back to Statesville.

I think I learned to take chances, gamble with my future—but not in the harmful way my father had done, not by calling his boss a fool or punching him out; or by telling my sisters and everyone else what a great country Russia was, a country about which he knew absolutely nothing. Some Commie had gotten to him in that Canadian foundry, my sisters said. I did learn from him, after all.

So much for early childhood.

In May 1933, when I was twelve, Mother and I rode two night trains from Statesville to Portsmouth, Virginia, talking a lot, sleeping a while, excited over the beginning of a new life. Mutt Napoleon, my first of many dogs, was unhappily trapped in the baggage car in a wooden crate built by a neighbor. Though steam trains swayed and jerked and pounded, sounding whistles and bells at major crossings, there was a magic to them, a power that rose from the huge driving wheels that carried us to the new life. Modern trains don't have a tenth of the character that coal-burners had.

There was a dining car in the first train but we ate from the wicker basket of the skinny boy in the brown uniform, topped by a hat with a shiny brass plate saying "Atlantic News Company." He would go up and down the aisle every half hour, yelling, "Candy, cookies, apples . . . " They worked most trains of the period, selling magazines and newspapers as well as edibles. I envied him, riding those wonderful trains. I later used him as a character model.

After six years without a regular job, my father had finally found work at the Norfolk Navy Yard, which is actually in Portsmouth. Fully qualified as a molder, his many firings over the years had left behind a bad employment record. Apparently, civil service personnel cared little about the past when hiring laborers at twenty-five dollars a week. And Mother hoped he'd learned his lesson. But she'd thought that at other times in Pennsylvania, Canada, North

Carolina, and Tennessee. We didn't know how many other places he'd worked.

Portsmouth dates back to 1608 when Captain John Smith, of *Pocahantas* fame, surveyed it. Among its temporary residents were Lord Cornwallis of the Revolutionary War, Andrew Jackson, Henry Clay, Benedict Arnold, and Robert E. Lee. Behind old walls and along a few brick sidewalks are residences that can also be found in such historic Southern cities as Georgetown, Alexandria, Charleston, and Savannah. Portsmouth figured in with the Confederacy. The *Merrimac* had gotten her iron armament in the Navy Yard. There's a Confederate statue on Court Street which I used in *A Sailor Returns,* 2001. We were entering hallowed ground.

A few miles outside of Portsmouth, on the southeast corner, is Cradock, built in 1918 to house blue-collar workers of World War I. Cradock and the downstairs rooms of one of those wooden, war-built houses was our destination by streetcar. I'd never been so excited. Another state; a town near water, near ships. Nappy was now in my lap as we bucked and pitched along. I've probably been companion to twenty dogs in my lifetime.

We passed the fences of the sprawling Navy Yard, the largest in the country, that Sunday morning, and I could see in the distance the great ships that were tied up where my father worked. I could see the world-famous hammerhead crane, capable of lifting the heaviest guns on earth. Somewhere in me is a considerable dollop of salt, from an unknown past, perhaps a great-great-great grandfather sailing out of Hamburg or Bremen; I'd had the hankering of water long before we moved to Virginia. I remember asking my father that day if we could have a boat. He said yes without the slightest idea where that money would originate. He was like that, making penniless promises. Twenty-five dollars a week starting pay?

The north boundary of Cradock was Paradise Creek, a shallow, muddy, winding estuary that smelled like anything but Paradise at low tide. It was inhabited by herons, gudgeons, and crabs. I was to spend summer days on it, crabbing. With the help of my father, I rebuilt a rowboat and used rotten fish heads for bait. I sold the steamed crabs for a nickel each.

The streetcar clicked across the wooden bridge and then we were in Cradock, named after a British admiral killed in late World War I. The town was, and is, a unique place, laid out with a street plan shaped like an anchor. It is one of the first communities in America designed for self-containment, historically recognized as home of the first planned shopping center in America. Around Afton Square were grocery stores, a drugstore, a barber shop, a fish market, a bakery, a cleaners, a fire station, and a community hall. It was playwright Thornton Wilder's classic "Our Town," but in the South. From first sight I had a love affair with Cradock.

One had the feeling of going onto a college campus or a military reservation. On Afton Square was a bandstand and a big World War I cannon. That square was the site of many teenage stickball games, played with half a tennis ball and broomsticks. It could have served as backdrop for another Norman Rockwell *Saturday Evening Post* cover.

There was a friendliness to the village from the moment we walked up from the streetcar line to our temporary quarters. My father had selected Cradock because it was a "workingman" place and he felt at home there. The man we rented from, who lived upstairs, was also employed at the shipyard.

Dawn to dark, there was enchantment that first summer in Virginia. When the wind was blowing southwest I could hear the "nine o'clock gun" from the Navy Yard. In a tradition dating back to 1847, the cannon fired every evening for tattoo with chronometrical precision. Generations of Portsmouth and Cradock children were to heed their mothers' warnings to be home by the nine o'clock gun. It gave a stability to the town, like the lamplighter's cry "All's well." Remarkably, all *was* mostly well.

Until school began I explored, a highly recommended and inexpensive activity for would-be writers of high school age. I followed the Norfolk and Western tracks down to the river, often hopping slow coaljacks for a ride, in order to watch the small freighters that chugged up the Elizabeth toward Norfolk on the Inland Waterway and to see oil tankers unloading at the refinery. I followed the streetcar tracks on foot into Portsmouth and prowled the waterfront warehouses to shouts of "Get away from here, boy." I was again practicing being alone, a big part of a writer's life.

Sometimes I just sat on a pier and watched boat and ship traffic, wanting to be on the river myself. I'd watch those ferry side-wheelers plying the mile or so to Norfolk. Sometimes I'd use a dime for round-trip fare to Norfolk and roam the waterfront from the ferry docks south to the fertilizer plant that processed menhaden fish meal, letting off an ungodly smell. I didn't realize I was storing up sights, sounds, and smells that I'd use later in *The Odyssey of Ben O'Neal,* 1977, a novel set on Cape Hatteras ocean banks and Norfolk river banks.

I first saw the Atlantic Ocean on a wintry Sunday afternoon. On the sands of Cape Henry, I was treated to a Coast Guard crew taking a lifesaving boat out through the breakers, ten seamen wielding long-sweep Viking oars. It is another of those special memories, like the Klansmen, as vivid today as it was more than a half century ago—the breakers, the boat, the wind, and the sea smell. It was the beginning of my lifelong romance with the sea, the setting of many of my books.

I remembered lying in my bed listening to the sounds of ships' steam whistles and air horns on the Elizabeth River when the wind blew out of the east. I'd been a young reader of sea stories, in book form or whenever the *Saturday Evening Post* decided to print a sailing adventure. I wanted to be on the outgoing tide for Java, Conakry, Capetown.

I stayed very busy during that humid summer before school began. My worst job was plucking chickens for a grocery store on serene Afton Parkway. Saturdays, I killed hens out behind the store with a hatchet, then tossed them into a big iron vat of boiling water, later gutting and defeathering them. Pay: fifty cents for the day.

Frozen chickens hadn't come on the market yet. Beheaded, spasming on the ground for five minutes, spurting blood, the victims finally unnerved me. The vat smell was gagging.

I soon quit and found a much superior job collecting plaster-of-paris tooth impressions for a group of dentists. Bag on my back, I'd take the ferry to Norfolk and deliver the impressions to a Granby Street lab. A week later, I'd go back to pick up the false teeth and deliver more impressions. Pay: two dollars for the round trip.

Sadly enough, lost forever are the teenage jobs of many small town yesterdays: cutting neighbors' lawns, pushing a two-wheeled mower instead of riding a gas-powered saddle, bustling around town as errand boys and Western Union boys and bicycle delivery boys and newspaper delivery boys, manning counters as soda jerkers. Girls have always cornered the babysitter market but expect high-tech electronic robot sitters by the time of hydrogen cars.

FALLING IN LOVE WITH TYPEWRITERS

"Can you write?" asked David "Pete" Glazer, sports editor of the Portsmouth, Virginia, *Star*, an evening newspaper with approximately eighteen thousand circulation. He was staring at me with cold suspicion. The year was 1934 and I'd just turned thirteen, ready to enter Cradock High School as a rosy-cheeked freshman.

"Yessir," said I, over the clack of several newsroom typewriters. I couldn't even write a proper letter much less a sports story. I was a terrible student and didn't want to be educated.

Earlier that week, Joe Goldberg, older than I was, had finished Cradock High and was about to enter college. He asked if I wanted his spare-time job. Joe lived six or seven blocks from me in our small village some six miles from the *Portsmouth Star* premises. I think he felt sorry for me, knowing my father was a laborer at twenty-five a week. I said I did. He said I would earn fifty cents a week covering any sports event in which our school teams, the Admirals, took part. Fifty cents was a small fortune then, the nation emerging like a starved turtle from the Great Depression. *So I began writing—for money.* Pure hot cash. Joe had recommended me highly, taking a considerable chance.

More than a half-century later Dr. Goldberg cannot remember

why he picked "Hayseed" Taylor to be his successor. I am forever grateful that he did. Neither do I have any idea who gave me the nickname, even before I entered high school, but it was without malice, I think.

Yes, I'd come to Norfolk County from the down-and-out, red clay region of North Carolina, and was indeed a hayseed from Statesville. Skinny, gangling, in too-short britches, I looked like a hick and talked like a hick and thought like a hick, and the supposedly more sophisticated Virginians, even the low-bred ones, decided that's what I was. They were correct.

I had, of course, wanted to be a hunting and fishing guide—not a newspaper writer. I couldn't imagine a better way to make a living than outdoors. College wasn't needed to catch fish.

I'd spent my Tarheel grammar school time gazing out the window and daydreaming, not studying, drawing World War I aerial combat pictures with canvas-clad British Spads shooting down canvas German Fokkers. I could spell my name. That was about all. My average grade during the erstwhile knee-pants years was an unstable "D." My handwriting was barely legible. But I did want the fifty cents. Cokes and Milky Ways were a nickel, as was the streetcar fare. Despite the Depression, life was wonderful.

Glazer said to bring him a page and a half of double-spaced, typed copy after the football games were over for the Sunday edition. So two young Jews started a Christian bumpkin out to be a writer. Pete, reviewing my first book years later, wrote, "He was the rawest recruit I'd ever had." That was indeed kind.

My father was persuaded to buy me a third- or fourth-hand L. C. Smith typewriter for several dollars at a Portsmouth pawn shop, an exact right place for an instrument that was to be used for journalistic larceny. Knowing my North Carolina school grade performances, he had a right to be surprised. He frowned, I remember. "*You're* going to work for a newspaper?" We brought the Smith home on the streetcar, not being able to afford a Ford, then or later. I have no idea where he got the money for the earlier shotgun or the typewriter. I think Mary might have helped with the typewriter money.

I was a bit frightened by Pete Glazer, who I assumed had gone to college. After all, he was an editor. My assumption was wrong. At twenty, he was self taught. He earned ten dollars a week at the *Star.* He loved the crazy newspaper business.

Suddenly I was in the world of adults. Small town newspapering *was* fun then, typewriter hunt and peck two-fingered, the men and a few women playing life games, having fun writing, smoking and drinking. I was entranced. They were storybook people and I was in total awe of them.

As a teenager Pete kicked off his journalistic career by covering boxing stories for the area newspapers, the cross-river Norfolk *Virginian-Pilot,* the *Ledger-Dispatch*, and the *Star.* No pay, just self-created opportunity. At eighteen, he was hired by the *Star* as a general reporter and achieved the sports editor slot some months later.

I also got involved in the amateur boxing world a year later, not as a fighter but as a cornerman wielding a sponge to a group of "Simon-pures" between the three-minute gongs. My best friend and neighbor Louis Bass had started a career as a fighter in the lightweight division when he was fourteen and we were inseparable, a Damon and Pythias relationship. I rubbed him down and loosened his muscles before a fight. I put on baseball catcher mitts so he could practice jabbing. Throughout high school I traveled with him to bouts mostly at the smoke-filled Ocean View Athletic Club, north of Virginia Beach. Hearing the crowd roar, toweling off his sweat at the one-minute break between rounds, sponging water into his mouth, I could almost feel every body or face punch that he took. Experience!

I was paid a dollar or two for my efforts as cornerman. *Anything legal to make money.* The experience was golden for a kid who hadn't started to shave. I soon wrote glowing stories about Lou for the *Star,* who was undefeated until he turned professional. I now tell students who want to write to get real-life experiences of any kind—except the cocaine variety.

I've often thought it was remarkable that teenagers like myself in the nineteen thirties and forties, and well before, could work around the edges of adult endeavors, make contributions, earn money, develop self esteem.

∽o∽

I well remember the forty-by-forty newsroom, with its alcove for the Associated Press and United Press teletype machines, no air conditioning. It smelled of wheat paste and tobacco, and from the dimly lit composing room next door there came the sound of the linotype machines making lead letters from a foul molten vessel called a "pig."

There were nine or ten of those machines, five or six always manned by operators who often had asthma or other respiratory diseases from the awful fumes. Most were chain-smokers as well, dooming themselves as I surely did. They were eye-glassed gnomes and to speak to them I had to shout. The *Star* became my miraculous school, the glib editors my teachers. I thought I needed no other school. I hung out there as much as possible.

All morning, big, sturdy typewriters were pecked away at by five sets of male hands. Four sets were white. One, black. Copy was ripped out of the Underwoods to be walked back to the composing room and converted into type. "Heads" for leading off the stories were also walked back. The managing editor, pint-sized Bob Barber, usually wrote the "banner," or major headline, to sweep across the top of the front page. Then it was deadline time, a glory-be time in the newsroom.

At about 2:30 P.M. there would be the rumble of metal cylinders in the press located behind the composing room, an equally shadowy area. Soon, the seven-day-a-week newspaper was rolling out, the thick black ink adding its heady smell to the publishing drama.

The ancient building even shook. I was in writer's heaven from the first day I heard the rumble and watched the folded papers slide out.

That particular press had once rolled in Havana for a dictator. Big-headed, big-bodied, smooth-talking publisher Norman Hamilton, soon to be a U.S. congressman, had bought it after an assassination. The press was in keeping with the *Star's* own unique personality. Hamilton, whom I used as "Henry Gladly" in *Walking Up a Rainbow,* 1994, wrote a Sunday column called "Barbecued Politics." Once he was chased around one of the Norfolk-Portsmouth ferries by an enemy with a cat-o-nine-tail whip, Hamilton's bushy white hair flying as he dodged between the cars and up and down the port and starboard passenger areas. Why invent fictional characters when so many real ones are available? The reporters laughed at him behind his back.

On rare occasions, such as Lindbergh's 1929 flight to Paris, the first aerial ocean crossing, or the death of a president or the beginning of a war, an "extra" would be published. Even the newsmen would hit the streets to "hawk" it, caught up in the excitement. I hawked several times, walking the streets yelling, "Extra! Extra!" Tingling excitement was what I felt when hanging around the newsroom, listening. I spent almost as much time there as I did at school. Just listening. With the invention of TV, "extras" vanished.

The newspaper building, circa 1878, was appropriately housed in a three-story former whiskey warehouse, the fading name "Mahoney Spirits" still visible on the facade. A courtroom dealing with crime and other county matters was on the second floor, and on the third floor was a walkway over to the Seaboard Airline railroad headquarters and station. Whenever there was maritime excitement on the adjoining muddy brown Elizabeth River—maybe an aircraft carrier or a battleship coming in—photographer Tommy Bie would climb up to the roof and pop away. Up I'd go with him, caught in the instant drama.

Diagonal across the foot of High Street were the Portsmouth-Norfolk ferry docks, nightly scene of raucous, drunken sailors on their return from Norfolk's naughty East Main Street to their ships at the Navy Yard several miles up river. Oh, the high-stacked, coal-burning ferries of my youth. Several had been built in the 1880s, propelled by thrashing side paddle wheels, cousins to Mississippi boats.

A block away from the *Star* was police headquarters and the city jail, soon to be haunts of mine. I talked to the cops and prisoners. One more block up, intersecting High Street, was Crawford Street, with its railroad spur and a fruit stand that sold red bananas and coffee beans from Cuba. Crawford was also the heart of the "red light," or prostitute, district. Sometimes I chatted with the "ladies of the night." Why not? I was learning to be a reporter. Opposite the jail and across the Seaboard rail tracks were the Issac Fass fish docks, lapped at by the dirty river. I enjoyed visiting and watching Atlantic catches being unloaded. I soaked it all up, wallowed in it. No teenager was having the fun I was having.

Inspired by the people-rich locale, the writers at the *Star*, and the sounds and smells of the newspaper—a living organism with a thudding heart—I fell in love with ink and words at that time. Desperately, hopelessly, eternally in love, there in Tidewater, Virginia, in a town that was rowdy underneath and had been that way back to Revolutionary days.

I used old Portsmouth as Evander Bryant's hometown in *A Sailor Returns*, 2001.

∽o∽

The first football game was scheduled for mid-September and here it was steaming mid-August and I didn't have the faintest idea how to report it. Daily I read the *Star* first page to last, giving special attention to the sports section. I'd done that before ever meeting Pete Glazer. My mother had taught me to read by the time I was five; the first book I put on my shelf was the thick *Action Adventure Bible Stories,* illustrated and in large print. When my father gave me that fishing pole at age three, my mother purchased the bible stories as a balance. I was a reader day and night and likely write action-adventure stories these days because of the bible book.

Joe Goldberg had gone somewhere with his family so I couldn't ask him for help. I wisely decided that the only way I could cover that first game, then, was to copy someone else. In telling Glazer I knew how to write, I'd already burned my bridge so I couldn't copy him. With cunning and foresight, I took a large yellow legal tablet and a half-dozen pencils, then took the ferry over to Norfolk and the *Virginian-Pilot* building.

William Cox, a fine sports writer-editor, usually began his Saturday afternoon football coverage for the *Pilot* with a weather report: "Under a clear blue, beautiful autumn sky, the University of Virginia defeated William and Mary, 6 to 0 . . . " He had a lead sentence for a rainy day, cloudy day, snowy day, misty day . . . Ah, a solution!

I copied down every single football story he'd written over the past year and labeled them—Sunny day, cloudy day, rainy day, snowy day, misty day . . . I was grossly cheating, of course.

The sun was out, sky blue, weather warm, the afternoon the Cradock Admirals played Norview and I lifted Mr. Cox's "sunny day" story from the pile and began copying, "Under a clear blue, beautiful autumn sky, the Cradock Admirals defeated Norview, 12 to 6 . . . " Writing larceny! Pure theft, out of necessity.

After watching the game, I pecked out the story on the L. C. Smith, then got on a borrowed bicycle and pedaled down to the barricaded Paradise Creek bridge with its big, red sign, "DANGER, UNSAFE." There, I lifted the wheels over the barricade and threaded around the rotten boards, then pedaled by the junkyard with its real dog, and finally got on the path by the trolley tracks and proceeded to the *Star* to collect my fifty cents. This would be the postgame route for the next three years, I hoped.

Glazer changed a few words for editorial clarity. And, suddenly, there I was, a cheating bylined writer, thirteen unspectacular years on earth. I fell back on William Cox for the rest of the gridiron season and similarly copied *Pilot* stories to report on basketball, track, and baseball. I now tell students that copying is a fine way to learn how to write if you copy good writers. "Sooner or later, you'll find your own style." See how words fit together in sentences and how you can make them say what you want them to say. Or try.

Glazer taught me as I went along, making corrections, always explaining why. His was a one-on-one journalism school; I don't think I could have learned more at Columbia University, an institution known for teaching the art of newspapering. I had a private, unpaid tutor throughout my four years of high school. "Tell it like it is," Pete said.

He said, "Go read Kipling." I did.

> *I keep six honest serving men*
> *(They taught me all I knew)*
> *Their names are What and Why and When*
> *And How and Where and Who*
> —*The Elephant's Child,* Rudyard Kipling

I hung around the newsroom whenever I could and soaked up the atmosphere, asking questions, trying to get my education there rather than in those dull halls of learning paid for with taxpayer funds. I failed at school most of the time, anyway, particularly math. I'm surprised I wasn't kicked out. I recognized that the quality of teachers, working for much less than a hundred a month, was superb. They had the respect and support of the community and I cannot remember a bad one. Neither can I remember a single student who could not read or write. It was my fault that I didn't learn math like the others.

The newsroom inhabitants were an often funny and unruly lot. The society editor was an imposing seventy-year-old lady who wrote her page with a pencil, causing Bob Barber eye-strain when he edited it. Lila came to work each day with a big cloth bag. In it was a pint of bourbon and she frequently went to the john with her bag, so by the time her workday was over she staggered. She called me "Sonny," always forgetting my name.

Due to my age, no one ever offered me a drink. But foolishly, at fifteen, I decided to join the adult world and lit up in public. I reached four packs a day at zenith—and eventually a surgeon's knife.

Puffing away, I sponged up the sights and the talk and the hee-haw laughter about the triumphs and frailties of humans. The reporters talked about such lovely things as local murder, sex scandals, politics, fighters, and the Portsmouth Cubs professional baseball team. They touched upon almost every facet of daily life—even Congressman Hamilton, making sure he wasn't listening. I hung on almost every delightful word.

Hamilton addressed me as "Boy," not knowing my name or caring about it. I was a cockroach to be stepped on. Teenagers should always have contact with a Hamilton. It is instructive for later in life when human cockroaches abound. On afternoons when we were both in the building at the same time, he often stood in his office doorway and pointed down to his brown shoes. He could have gone across the street to the Greyhound terminal and gotten a shine from the bootblack for fifteen cents. But I was on his payroll. He never thanked me.

I was always a good listener. I listened when bums, sometimes rail-riding hobos, came into the newsroom to tell their wild stories hoping to cadge a quarter, usually for muscatel wine. I listened when the town's Russian intellectual came in to talk about things no one understood. I eavesdropped on adult conversations about sex—that was always instructive. I went upstairs and listened while all sorts of cases were tried in court. Shootings and the like. I kept visiting the police station and talking to the cops and to the men and women behind bars. Learning, learning, without benefit of a classroom, knowingly denying myself college. My grades would not permit entry, anyway.

Soon, I covered pro wrestling over in Norfolk and pro fights in Portsmouth. By the end of my sophomore year I no longer needed to copy "professional" writers. I had my own style and method. No one, not even Pete Glazer, had caught my theft of words.

I remember particularly one afternoon at a football game in Cradock when my no-nonsense father dropped by the field before going to his homemade boat, an up-and-downer powered by a two-cylinder engine. The Admirals were playing South Norfolk that day and I was reporting for the *Star*, still earning my fifty cents, taking notes on a clipboard.

Four or five big bruisers from South Norfolk began harassing me. I probably weighed no more than 110 pounds, no match for any of them. Suddenly, out of nowhere, my father was there, between the bad guys and myself, slowly swinging a sealed bucket of prime-coat red lead paint. It likely weighed thirty or forty pounds and would have cracked skulls if he'd applied it. They melted away. Quickly. His gray eyes were deadly when he looked at me. His gaze seemed to be saying, "Don't take any crap from these bullies." He nodded to me and went on toward the Paradise Creek dock.

THE OUTER BANKS

Lacking a good imagination, certainly unable to write science fiction, I must rely on personal experience, research, and real characters to deliver my stories. Long hours of research usually go into any book, as well as travels to the source, domestic and overseas. Among my first books were stories of the North Carolina Outer Banks. I think I was still twelve when I first visited them that glorious first summer. Unknowingly, I began research on three books.

From our landlord I'd heard about those narrow fingers of barrier sand between the Atlantic Ocean and the sounds of North Carolina—Albemarle, Roanoke, Currituck, and Pamlico. He told me about the savage storms that had roared into them for hundreds of years, leaving more than a thousand shipwrecks scattered over many miles from the Virginia border south to Cape Lookout. The banks were truthfully called "The Graveyard of the Atlantic."

He told me about the wood-and-steel skeletons of the wrecks, the snow geese wintering grounds at Pea Island, the wild horses that roamed the beaches, the cottages built of shipwreck timbers and surrounded by whalebone fences. He told me about the hardy people who lived in the few villages between Oregon Inlet and Hatteras. Beyond the inlet there were no paved roads, just sand trails. It was said that the remote villages were a hundred years behind the rest of America. That was fine with me.

I sat between my father and our landlord at dawn in a battered old Chevy truck as we crossed the bridge over Albemarle Sound and put the tires on Outer Banks sand, turning south at Kitty Hawk. We were headed toward the inlet to fish for blues or flounder or anything else that would bite.

Soon, to the right were Kill Devil Hills where the Wright Brothers had made the world's first successful aircraft flight on December 7, 1903. I looked over at the dunes with awe. The landlord promised we'd stop on the way back so I could stand where the Wrights took off.

A little later, at the Oregon Inlet landing I met my first Outer Banker, Captain Toby Tillett, who became the "Jabez" Tillett of the *Hatteras Trilogy*. His bargelike wooden ferry was fifty feet long, with room for eight vehicles, as I remember. In *Stranger from the Sea*, set in 1898, I describe Jabez as "stringy as a wreck pole . . ." with "an Adam's apple like a channel rock." That's how Captain Tillett looked to me that early morning.

He talked in that peculiar Devon English dialect: Tide was "toide" and many was "slew" and "swayzed" was something that moved around. Supposedly, the Banks were first inhabited by a few Indians of the Hatterisk tribe, and then by shipwreck survivors from Devon in about the late sixteenth century.

Tillett was once again a character model, like old skinflint Norman Hamilton, of *The Star*. I can't think of any novel which is not populated by people I've either met or researched.

It didn't take long to cross the inlet and drive out to the lonely beach. North or south there wasn't a human to be seen. It was low tide and the sand was hard-packed. We went south along the edge of the surf for a few miles. Near Pea Island I saw the snow goose wintering grounds and then a herd of small wild horses with huge hoofs, descendants of Arabian stock shipwrecked a century before. They galloped along the water, frightened by the truck engine.

At last we parked and broke out the fishing rods, then seined for sand crabs to use for bait. After maybe an hour, getting no strikes, I gave up on fishing and explored the driftwooded beach. I was attacked by diving terns at one point, a scene I used later in both *The Cay* and the Outer Banks stories.

Soon I found the sun- and wind-whitened exposed ribs of a ship, likely a schooner or a barkentine that had wrecked in the 1800s. How many sailors had been on it? How many had died in the pounding surf? When and how it wrecked? Buried beneath the sands where I walked were other skeletons along with their secrets. The writer in me was filled with questions.

But, of course, I had no idea that I'd ever become a writer and eventually tell the half-true stories of fictional Ben O'Neal and a little British girl named "Teetoncey" (meaning "teeny-tiny" in Outer Banks language of the day). The O'Neal families still live on the Banks, as do the Midgetts, the Meekins, the Scarboroughs, the Fulchers, and others with Devon names. They were fishermen and gallant lifesavers, rowing surf boats into raging waters to rescue real-life Teetonceys.

My own mother served as the model for Rachel O'Neal, Ben's mother. She was "a thin woman with a large nose and gray hair." Mother, of course, was a deeply religious woman as was Rachel O'Neal.

I returned to the Banks during high school to fish and hang out when I was beginning to learn how to write at the *Star*. I explored fearsome Cape Hatteras—later known as "Torpedo Junction" during World War II—always looking toward shore from a tanker bridge. I have a mental scrapbook of places around the world.

Much later, while working in New York, I heard that weathered driftwood was being sold at art galleries on 64th Street. It was now, of all things, "art." In my teens I'd known where tons of it could be found—south of Oregon Inlet. So I drove down there with an artist, rented a World War II army command car, and crossed on the same ferry of fifteen years earlier in search of driftwood. Captain Toby

Tillett was still the skipper. Not far from Chicamacomico Lifesaving Station, the engine stopped and we had to be towed out of the surf by the Coast Guard.

Night drawing near, accommodations were limited at the station and I slept in the same bed as Chief Petty Officer Filene Midgett, commander of the unit. A huge, rough man, his snoring was loud enough to chase away any "ghostie" of the Banks. I didn't sleep all night. He became the "Filene Midgett" of the *Outer Banks Trilogy,* both in appearance and manner. Use real people, I say.

Slowly but surely, again not really apparent to me at the time, I was gathering material for a novel. But it was not until I spent almost two weeks at the University of North Carolina that I came across the final piece of research that would tie the stories together. Intense research is my savior with all of the books.

UNC has a superb Outer Banks collection, and buried in the many documents was the story of a British barkentine that ran aground during a storm south of Chicamacomico. On board was a British family going from Barbados to New York City.

The Appletons survived the grounding as did everyone else on board, not a good start for any adventure book. So I killed Mrs. Appleton by bashing her head against a bulwark, then drowned Mr. Appleton as he was trying to swim ashore with the daughter. That left me with Wendy Lynn Appleton ("Teetoncey") washed up on shore unconscious, half-dead, to be discovered by Ben O'Neal and his yellow Labrador, Boo Dog, modeled after our family Labrador. So begins *Stranger from the Sea,* 1973. *Box of Treasures* and *Into the Wind* continue the story of Ben and Tee, which ends in their marriage and a baby named "Ben."

I think and hope that the *Outer Banks Trilogy* presents a rather true reflection of life as it occurred from Kitty Hawk to Cape Hatteras village at the turn of the century.

LEAVING HOME

I didn't graduate from high school. My fault again. To avoid humiliation, I had my picture in the yearbook, bought the class ring, even wore the cap and gown at the graduation ceremony, but the diploma wasn't signed. The kindly principal let it all happen but wouldn't affix his signature. I never passed freshman math. In fact, I didn't want to pass freshman math. Of course, I couldn't go on to college that fall of 1938 which dismayed sister Mary but bothered me not. I was already a bylined writer and didn't need college. Or so I thought.

With my father finally producing income, Mary had left Statesville to go to New York and was working as a secretary for a Broadway stage producer. She had me enroll in the Fork Union Military Academy, Fluvanna, Virginia, so I could be tutored in math. She thought the military discipline would focus me. I told her it was a waste of her money. I did get a break in the tuition by becoming a sports correspondent for the *Washington Post* and the *Washington Evening Star*, reporting by wire after every football game. After three months I departed, having passed high school math, at last, just to get it over with.

With Mother's "go for it" approval, I hitchhiked to Washington and applied for copyboy jobs at the *Post, Star, Herald,* and Scripps-Howard *Daily News,* a fast seven-editions-a-day tabloid. Copyboys were errand boys, lowest position on the staff. Due to today's word processors there are no longer paste pots to keep filled, no copy to "run" back to the composing room, no tearing off of takes from the AP and UPI teletype machines, no editor's coffee cups to be filled, no chores of a half-dozen lowly categories such as shining editor's shoes. At the time, most of the copyboys (none were girls) were college graduates seeking to land a newspaper job of *any* kind. I couldn't compete. I'd even tossed away my unsigned high school diploma. What good was it?

I suppose I did have a modicum of intelligence by then, despite my lack of credentials. I'd saved a sheaf of bylined stories from the *Portsmouth Star* and *Norfolk County News,* and lately from the *Washington Post* and *Star.* They'd be my aces, I decided, and I would plunk them down even before the city editor could ask about colleges and universities. I'd say I had four years of experience in newspapers and knew all about a city room. I wouldn't let him ask many questions. Overwhelm him!

Returning home for a weekend, I damaged a knee playing touch football, slipping on a cow pie. The timing was terrible. The *Daily News* had left a message at my boarding house. A copyboy job was open. I went back to Washington on crutches via the Chesapeake Bay boat and the city editor was most impressed, the skinny kid traveling all the way from Portsmouth for a job that paid eleven dollars weekly. I was seventeen.

From the day I went to work at the *Daily News* I had only one thing in mind: being upgraded to full reporter status. I went around and begged assignments, but the only taker was the drama editor. He let me review new films and summer theatre, keeping professional productions for himself. I was grateful, knowing that the managing editor read his own paper, front to back. *He'd notice the new byline,* I thought. I began interviewing show biz personalities.

My real target was a stocky, stubby, block-faced man named Rocky Riley, the sports editor. He had a well-deserved reputation of being the meanest editor in the newsroom. Gruff, impatient, profane, nonetheless he was a fine writer and wielded his editing pencil with exceptional skill. On most occasions, people don't learn from nice people. They learn from mean ones, one way or another. I often shined his shoes, Norman Hamilton revisited. Rocky Riley was an excellent teacher.

His star reporter was named Robert Ruark, another North Carolinian, a graduate of Chapel Hill who'd begun his career at the *News* as a copyboy. He worshiped Ernest Hemingway, modeling himself after the writer—even to the brush mustache and slouch hat. Ruark was later, after World War II, to become a best-selling novelist who enraged American women by writing that they didn't know how to make love. He suffered an untimely death just when his career was taking off. Ruark was known around town for his breezy style in his daily column. He was fun to read. I became friendly with him, using the North Carolina ties, and after I was on the job for five or six months he wrote a column entitled *Office Boy Staff Harbors Budding Fight Manager.* The lead paragraph read, "All unbeknownst to the good folk in the office, The *Daily News* is harboring a fight manager in its bosom. He isn't exactly a full-blown fight manager, rather more of an embryo bandit. He is sort of studying to be a fight manager as other young men practice to be President."

I quote more of his column because it was uncannily true: "Ted is unique among most young fight managers. He is the proud owner of Lou Bass, a product of the amateurs with some eighty fights behind him. They have been together six years. When Bass gets tagged, Ted's jaw aches for days . . .

"Taylor has embraced everything in the fight racket from being a bucket boy in Virginia fight clubs to fist-wrapper to promoter." Lou and I had grown up together. I loved him like a brother.

Ruark ended the column, "We do not see how he can ever become a useful member of society. Failing success as a handler of pugs, the poor guy wants to become a sports writer."

After the column was published, I decided to put pressure on Rocky Riley, week after week begging him to let me do a byline piece on any sports subject he chose. Finally, one afternoon he said, "There's a Greek boy over at Catholic University who just won the collegiate middleweight championship. Go talk to him and bring me the story Monday."

Calling the sports office at Catholic U., I arranged a time, then took a notebook and proceeded to do the interview. The boxer was a human ape, with hair matted on his chest, his back, his belly, and his legs—not unlike Lou Bass. He was also Phi Beta Kappa. I did not tell him I was a copyboy. He took me to be a full-fledged reporter, though he commented that I was "awfully young" to be writing for *The Daily News.*

Since this was a Friday afternoon, I had all weekend to create the masterpiece that would elevate me rather quickly to Rocky Riley's staff, alongside Robert Ruark. I went by the office to borrow a big Webster's dictionary and then to a typewriter place on 6th Street to rent a portable.

I wrote and rewrote all day Saturday and part of Sunday, proudly handing my three-page, double-spaced story to Rocky Riley on Monday. He read the first paragraph, frowned at me, and then balled the paper up and threw it across the room, narrowly missing the city editor. I was speechless.

He did not talk to me for three weeks. He communicated by handclaps and sign language to relay that he needed copy run to the composing room or wanted coffee in his cup or his shoes shined, or any other number of chores that came to his mind. I was never so low in spirit in all my short life. I thought I was washed up at age eighteen.

Finally he called me over, saying, "Look, kid, if you want to learn how to write, learn how to do it *simply*. I don't even know what the hell 'accoutrement' means."

My lead sentence in the story of the hairy boxer had read, "An erudite gentleman with a hirsute accoutrement . . . " I had cobbled it together out of Webster's.

From that day on, I have tried to write simply for both young readers and adults. I'm forever grateful for the lesson that the mean late Rocky Riley taught me. I hope heaven let him in. I use Webster's only to confirm spelling. If I don't know a word I don't use it.

∾o∾

Pete Glazer, my teacher at the *Portsmouth Star* who'd said I was the rawest recruit he'd ever had (I was his third recruit but agree I was the rawest), phoned me one morning in early summer, 1941, to say he was going into the Navy. He was about to be drafted and wanted no part of the Army and its muddy foot soldiers. He was bred and born in a Navy town.

I was still at the *Washington Daily News*, happily earning my eleven dollars a week, living on a forced diet of two meals a day. I was still doing theatre reviews on my own time, and still trying to persuade Rocky Riley to elevate me from threadbare copyboy to bylined sports reporter. He said he didn't need me, foul but wonderful man that he was.

Pete said, "You want to come back here and be sports editor? Bob (Barber, the managing editor) has said okay."

Sports editor? "Take your place?"

"Yeah."

"Pete, I don't know how to make-up a page." That was something well beyond reporting football or fights. That took judgment. I'd have to measure space; write heads. I remember hesitating. I clearly wasn't qualified.

"I'll show you. You want the job?"

It all happened too fast that morning. I had never been a full-fledged reporter much less an editor. Then I recalled that Pete had started at eighteen. He said, "The guys'll help you."

I thought a moment more and said, "Give me a week and I'll be down there."

Filling paste pots, running wire copy to various editors, taking copy to the composing room, filling coffee cups, shining Riley's shoes, and answering to the cries of "copyboy!" hadn't taught me very much, but being around those high-caliber, experienced editors had been worth it. The energy of seven *Daily News* editions a day, the speed devoted to getting them out, had been worth it. There were probably hundreds, if not thousands, of college journalism students who would have gladly changed places with me for five dollars a week.

At the time, Washington, with President Roosevelt in the White House, was suddenly an exciting city. War was raging in Europe. Bells rang constantly in the "wire room" where the press association machines clacked out copy. I was caught up in the war news and fed off it.

My parents had moved away from Cradock. My father had worked at the Navy Yard for eight years, the longest continued employment of his entire life, winding up with wages of fifty dollars a week. But he remained true to himself, arguing with bosses and co-workers, unable to shake off whatever demons had been chasing him for almost half a century. His retirement on disability had not been a sudden thing. While I was still in high school, he'd gotten me to write a letter to the chief of civilian workers at the Yard, claiming he'd injured his back in the foundry. Injured his back? That back could have held up a bridge.

I believe that the civil service people and his immediate bosses said, "By all means, get him out of here." Simultaneously, he applied for his Spanish American War pension. He would never work again, which I resented deeply. My sisters and I only hoped that my long-suffering mother wouldn't have to suffer in Melbourne, Florida. He bought a house for nine hundred dollars. We children would help, if we could.

My respect for my father fell another notch. There weren't many notches left. A war was surely coming on and he was an excellent iron molder. He owed his country. He owed my mother. It made no difference to him.

∞∾

I was now making fifteen dollars a week as sports editor and staff reporter, an improvement of four dollars over the *Daily News*. There were some other advantages. I was assigned to cover the weekly lunches of the local service clubs, reporting on their guest speakers. The Lion and Rotary-Kiwanis-type clubs always provided lunch for the press. I lunched free five days a week.

Lessons came early. I was boarding again and would take the city bus east down High Street toward the *Star* office every morning about eight o'clock. I tried to be observant on this ride while thinking about what I'd do at the typewriter until late afternoon. I had big shoes to fill.

En route to the *Star* building there were several gas stations on High Street, and one of them had a black bear to drum up business. Gas then was fourteen or fifteen cents a gallon, I believe. The station owners were highly competitive. The black bear station was on a corner and, as the bus stopped for a red light, it appeared to me that the owner was beating his animal. I was instantly furious but did not leave the bus to investigate. As soon as I got to the office I angrily pecked out a story about the bear being mistreated. It ran on the front page, *vox populi*, voice-of-the-people reportage.

Next morning, the gas station owner came into the newsroom *with his bear*, shouting, "Who the hell wrote that story?"

Bill Brown was at his typewriter up front, in his summer straw hat, and pointed to me, with a grin on his face.

Coming to my desk, the gas station owner shouted, "Look at this," and the bear lovingly kissed him on the mouth. I really thought he was going to punch me. I learned that morning to always get off the bus, or out of the car, and up from underneath it, and get the facts straight. Only one other time have I done a piece of unfactual work—I reported a pilot dead after his plane crashed in Dismal Swamp. In fact, he walked out with just a few facial scratches. The pilot was not happy with me, either.

My last big embarrassment at the *Star* came about because I was a weekly burlesque devotee. The advertising department gave away free passes to carnivals, circuses, sports events, and the Gayety Theatre over on East Main Street in Norfolk. I'd attend when a new feature act came to town. Burlesque in those days was innocent, no stripping down to the ultimate buff, and it served as a training ground for such name comics as Red Skelton, Milton Berle, and Red Buttons. Not quite nineteen years old, both healthy and curious, I had an immense interest in the female form.

I attended one evening after Miss Southern began her two-week run at the Gayety. She glided onstage in a lovely purple gown and began her stripping prance, continuing until she was down to pasties front and rear. The pasties held tassels of about eight inches in length. As the five-piece pit orchestra segued into another number, Miss Southern began to rotate the front tassels in a clockwise fashion; then turning her bottom to the audience she got the back tassels going, also clockwise.

Stunned, I'd never seen anything like this performance. I couldn't figure how she was doing it. The orchestra segued again and she got those tassels, both front and rear, going counter-clockwise. I couldn't believe her undulating dexterity. The side view was equally amazing.

There's a good story here, I thought. Contacting the Gayety manager, I asked for an interview and soon stood outside Miss Southern's dressing room. Covering journalistic bases, I started with biographical data—born in Hertford, N.C., twenty-four years old—then got down to what I really wanted to know: "How do you make the tassels rotate?" I asked.

"I don't exactly know. I just do my shoulder this way and I do my bottom that way."

I was taking notes furiously. But a little "shoulder movement" and a "little bottom movement" did not and could not explain what was happening on that stage. Two nights later, I went through the whole thing again with her without success.

Back in the newspaper office the next day, the story I wrote dodged the issue and I didn't even submit it to Bob Barber. I had not explained sufficiently what Miss Southern really did with her tassels. That evening I checked the shelves of the rather good library at the boardinghouse and *Learning Physics* caught my eye.

I scanned the book and there was what seemed to be the perfect solution, framed in a scientific way. *Force and counter-force.* I was quite satisfied now and the story appeared, along with the stripper's picture, in the Sunday edition. My satisfaction lasted a few days until a letter from a physics professor at William and Mary College arrived. He made me appear to be a dunce. *Force and counter-force!* The letter was printed the following Sunday.

I learned Lesson II: Never fake research. Some books have been clocked at sixty percent research, forty percent writing, so I always consult a variety of sources.

∽∞∾

Indian summer, a glorious time in Virginia. The sky was pure blue and the early frost had turned the leaves gold. Summer gardens were browning. The air was crisp until the sun was high. I remember how good my childhood had been; remember hunting in the corn fields for rabbits with the pale ivory stalks stripped of their husks, there to stand until spring plowing; remember the chimney smoke of the season's first fires. Good days, good smells, good writing for me.

On Sunday afternoon, December 7, 1941, I had a casual romance going. My girlfriend had been a classmate at Cradock High and we'd been going together about six months. With hair the color of chestnuts, nice smile, good body, we had low-budget fun.

In the midst of what was then known as "necking" on the sofa in her parents' front room, the radio interrupted a Tommy Dorsey song: *Pearl Harbor has been bombed by Japanese carrier forces . . .*

I grabbed my coat and was out the door in seconds, running down Gillis Road to the bus stop on Afton Parkway. Already on that quiet, chill Sabbath afternoon people were coming out of their houses, shocked at the news, wanting to talk.

As soon as the bus arrived in Portsmouth, I sprinted to the *Star* building. Both Bob Barber and Bill Brown were there. The printing plant foreman had been called to round up his typesetters and pressmen. The *Star* would have an EXTRA on the streets within hours, and we'd go out to shout, "Extra, extra, Pearl Harbor bombed!"

This was exactly what I liked about the newspaper business: sudden events that pounded pulses. A human drama that had begun halfway around the world had touched this small city, and would keep on touching it again and again for years to come.

The largest naval shipyard in the United States was less than two miles away. Pete Glazer had gone there the moment he heard the flash. The radio was on in the newsroom. What about sabotage? Were the Germans about to strike here? They'd already torpedoed the Portsmouth-based destroyer *Kearny* in October.

Across the river was a naval air station, the largest naval operating base on the East Coast. Thousands of personnel and dozens of ships from Portsmouth and Norfolk would be involved in the coming conflict.

Barber sent me to the police station. Detectives were going to raid the three Japanese restaurants and cart the owners and cooks to jail. Nine months earlier the FBI had given the local police the names of all the Japanese residing and working in Portsmouth. As I climbed into the front seat of a squad car, siren screaming and red roof light revolving, heading for the first restaurant, not far from the

Navy Yard gate, I knew exactly why I'd chosen to become a newspaperman.

Not long into January, I interviewed the thirteen survivors of the Esso tanker *Allen Jackson* at Norfolk's naval base. They hadn't been out of the water twenty-four hours yet, and they sat dazed on bunks in sick bay. Twenty-two others had drowned or were burnt to death when their ship was torpedoed off Cape Hatteras by a German submarine. Death, said several of the survivors, seemed to follow them away from the *Jackson* through a ring of flaming oil. They could hear the screams of their shipmates burning alive. I grew up during that one interview.

The *Jackson* sinking was my first war story. I'd never before dealt with death and think I'd only seen one corpse up to that time. As the survivors recounted what had happened not long after midnight, when most were asleep, I had trouble comprehending what they'd gone through and putting it down with accuracy—the blast of the two torpedoes, the huge explosions, the roaring fire. I did not know that later I would have a personal connection—I rode a tanker in sub waters.

Captain Felix Kretchmer said, "After the explosions I found myself on the bathroom floor. Flames were coming in through my bedroom door and the cabin portholes. I squeezed myself through the bathroom porthole though my body was too large to go through. I can't explain how I did it. As the vessel broke up, the suction carried me away from the bridge ladder. With the help of a couple of small boards I was able to keep afloat in the warm Gulf Stream until I was picked up seven hours later by the destroyer *Roe* . . . "

I still have the story in a scrapbook. I wrote down what they told me, without embellishment, as stark and dramatic as they had said it, captain down to mess boys. I learned it was the right way to report a story, then and now. The shock on their drawn faces, their tired voices told me they weren't embellishing. Keep the words simple and clean. Thanks Rocky Riley.

Over the next two months, I covered merchant ship sinkings off the coast, defense and black-out stories, and once rode with the FBI. Sports was a minor subject now, and I used "canned" stories, mostly features, from the Associated Press and United Press, to fill those pages.

∞∞

On a Saturday afternoon in late January, a time when all of us in the newsroom would scan the Sunday edition for any stop-the-press horrific errors, Bill Brown, looking over the society pages, said, "Hey, Ted, you made the society page."

"I did what?" I crossed to his desk. He was grinning and point-ing to an item that said I was engaged to be married. At age twenty, I let out a wounded cry. *I was too young to be married. I had some liv-ing to do first. I could be a father in less than a year!*

My casual girlfriend had mentioned marriage several times and I'd parried as best I could: I'd have to go into service soon, I said. I'd registered for the draft. I didn't have the money for marriage, I said. Truthfully, I wasn't all that much in love. "Let's wait 'til the war is over. Let's talk about it some more." I might have even said some-thing like "I love you," which led to this January surprise. Frankly, I hated to be squeezed over such a momentous subject.

GOING TO WAR

I asked the girl with hair the color of chestnuts why she did it. She replied that she thought it would be a nice surprise, using the newspaper to tell everyone, all of her friends and mine, that we were going to be married. She'd conspired with the new society editor, a relative of hers.

Having no known physical defects aside from still being a 120-pound rail at six feet, more bones than flesh, I knew that the Army or Navy or Coast Guard would gladly enfold me. Meanwhile I selfishly wanted to partake of some of life's goodies prior to gallantly sacrificing myself on some far-flung battlefield or in some icy ocean, killed by either the Nazis or the Japanese.

New York had been on my mind since the draft had begun to uncaringly scoop up both the fittest and the unfittest. Sisters Mary and Eleanor were working up there, I reasoned. Mary was still secretary to the Broadway producer and Eleanor was an editor at Dell publishing.

War and the wedding announcement from the chestnut-haired girl levered me into quitting the *Star* and buying a ticket for a train ride north. My plans were to apply to the newly-founded U.S. Merchant Marine Academy on Long Island, then find a temporary job and wait until my body was claimed for sea service. I'd sail freighters and tankers, always a goal.

Sleeping on Mary's couch in Greenwich Village, I went around each day filling out applications at the *New York Times,* the *Herald Tribune,* the *Daily News,* and the *Mirror,* hoping I could land a temporary job doing whatever. The personnel people weren't overly impressed that I'd been sports editor of the *Portsmouth Star.* Was it a weekly? "You don't look old enough to be an editor of anything!" one said.

Then one day my British brother-in-law, who had a radio show, said, "I talked to the personnel manager at NBC about you. Go see him tomorrow." There was a job open in publicity. NBC was losing workers to the services weekly, and I was soon hired to tap out press releases about the soap operas at thirty-five dollars a week, a fortune at the time. I reported to network headquarters in Rockefeller Center.

The office resembled the city room of the *Daily News,* even to a copy editor, and the occupants of the twenty-odd desks—all blasé New Yorkers—were much older than I was. Staying late the first two or three nights, I examined the stories they had written. Some seemed tired. Much relieved, I thought I could compete. Oh, the gall of youth. It was different writing, a style I'd never done.

I rented a one-bedroom furnished apartment on East 34th Street. After the fourth week of publicizing the soaps, I was summoned to the NBC personnel office and asked if I knew anything about Bill Stern. Of course I did. He was the preeminent radio sportscaster of the land, an early John Madden. He did football and blow-by-blow fight broadcasts from Madison Square Garden. My kind of man. He also did a nightly fifteen-minute network show for a shaving cream sponsor. He was losing his scriptwriter to the Army. Did I think I could write radio for Mr. Stern? Personnel, examining my employment form, had seen that I'd been a sports editor.

Luck again! *Pure, absolute, unbelievable luck.* Seventy-five a week now. I could take my sisters and brothers-in-law out to dinner. I could go to nightclubs. I could have a good seat at a Broadway show. I was suddenly back in sports. I called Lou Bass in Washington and Pete Glazer in the Navy Yard. I would have called my parents except they had no phone. I called sisters Louise and Naoma. My feet barely touched the sidewalks between Rockefeller Center and 34th Street.

I didn't know how long it would last and I was beginning to feel uncomfortable in civilian clothes as I walked around town. I should be in the war. The newspapers were filled with combat stories; the radio networks were constantly updating Americans about the fighting in the Pacific and in Europe. Though skinny, I was healthy enough to be in battle. I'd work with Stern, get that astonishing salary, until called for national duty.

I studied the scripts of the previous writer. Basically, there was an updating of sports news and scores plus several feature stories. Writing for the ear did not seem all that different than writing for the eye. Again, I was learning.

I wrote Stern's scripts for five months before I received the letter announcing I'd been accepted for officer training at King's Point, New York, out on Long Island. If I passed the Navy physical I would become a deck cadet, shipping out after three months indoctrination. Upon completion of training, I could sit for a third mate's license and become eligible for a commission as an ensign in the naval reserve. By this time I wanted to write about ships and the sea and the war, the great convoys that carried supplies overseas to the Allied soldiers and aircraft, and the German submarines that sought to destroy them.

I had a problem. I weighed one hundred twenty pounds and the Navy's requirement for officer training was one hundred twenty-eight pounds. Mary's husband was a Yale graduate and sent me to that institution's club. The athletic trainer told me to make a date with a Navy hospital corpsman at 90 Church Street, and be first on the scales that particular morning.

The trainer said, "Okay, you're going to be at 90 Church at seven o'clock. Right?"

I nodded.

"Set your alarm for four o'clock and start eating bananas and drinking thick ale. Above all, no matter how much it hurts, don't pee. Take a cab, not the subway, to 90 Church."

At approximately six seconds after seven o'clock in the morning I stepped off the scales weighing one hundred twenty-nine pounds. On the seventh second, I was urinating a yellow streak on my way to the head, Navy terminology for bathroom. The corpsman handed me a mop and bucket. I haven't had even a sip of thick ale ever since.

About two weeks later, suitcase in hand to soon stow civvies, I took the Long Island Railroad to Great Neck. The Merchant Marine Academy, its grounds bordering Long Island Sound, was less than a year old, and every building on this former movie magnate's estate was occupied, his mansion used as headquarters. A group of salty instructors had been assembled. An attempt was being made to pattern the place after Annapolis.

Like most other deck cadets, I struggled with the courses meant to teach me how to become a basic seaman and not screw up entirely on my first ship. Three months passed like three weeks and I left there looking like a junior officer but feeling like an apprehensive Sea Scout. By that time, chill winds were flowing across the Sound, causing shivers at outdoor morning assemblies. All of us thought about being torpedoed in the North Atlantic.

Chilling words crossed the Academy grounds. Already there were reports of cadets recently assigned to their first ships being killed in the U-boat battles.

Soon, it came my time to go to war.

∽∘∽

As an insignificant gill-green apprentice, I'd been assigned to serve aboard an old gasoline tanker, the SS *Harry F. Sinclair,* a ship that had already survived the flames of one torpedoing.

Not until much later did I know the details of what exactly had happened to her off the North Carolina coast at dawn April 5, 1942. The Coast Guard reported: "Five lookouts were on duty when a torpedo was seen to leap out of the water and hit beneath the pump room. The midship house was immediately engulfed in flames and nine men, including all the deck officers, were burnt to death. No. 2 boat was launched but those in it perished in the blazing water." Would I repeat this?

Having an honest gut fear of being blown up and roasted, I'd wanted to sail on fast freighters, in fast convoys, happily running away from the U-boats in this late autumn of 1942. I'd heard first-hand about the tanker war: Doenitz, the Nazi submarine admiral, had ordered his skippers to "Kill the tankers! Kill the tankers!" Doenitz meant to cut the lifeline of oil and gas to England so he could defeat the Allies. Tankers were already being destroyed faster than they could be built. I remembered my interview with the *Jackson* survivors.

I met Captain Ryti, master of the *Sinclair,* in a room at the Lord Baltimore Hotel and he told me where I could find his vessel. He said we'd probably load high octane in the Caribbean. *Great,* I thought. *Die swimming in flames.*

With an outlandishly high smokestack, the *Sinclair* looked every one of her twenty-five years the first time I saw her in the shipyard where she'd been repaired. It would be a few weeks before she was declared ready to sail, Ryti had said. Without cargo, she sat high out of the water, bow projecting into the gray Maryland sky. It was duck weather.

No one was aboard that cold morning and I prowled her from the paint locker, at the bow beneath the anchor windless, to the steering engine tucked beneath the stern deck plating aft of the steam turbine plant and boilers. It is strange, at times eerie, to explore an empty ship, particularly one where death has occurred. I climbed the forty-five-foot foremast ladder and entered the crow's nest, a steel tube lookout post with an entry door and roof. I was to spend hours over the next eighteen months up there searching for subs.

About four feet in diameter, a lookout crow's nest is constructed of steel, with the roof resembling an inverted pie tin. You can look 320 degrees, but it is unusable in heavy rain or fog and extremely cold in sub-Arctic waters. Soon I enjoyed the enclosure, climbing up the steel ladder, timing my steps to the ship's rise and fall in heavy seas—I'd scramble up a few feet when the hull rose and hang on when she went head down between waves.

The ship smelled of fresh paint and welding acids as I explored the bridgehouse, where I'd bunk with another cadet, and then the afterhouse, finally going below into the dimly lit engine spaces. Soon she was to come alive with mates, engineers, and civilian crew. U.S. Naval personnel would handle the machine guns, fore and aft, as well as the large 4.50 gun at the stern.

She was 432 feet length overall and could carry 78,310 barrels of gasoline in her sixteen tanks, which were beneath the catwalk that extended from her stern housing to the bridgehouse, then to the bow. Much later, I used her as the character model for the doomed SS *Tuttle* in *To Kill the Leopard,* 1993, an adult novel of World War II tanker warfare.

As I walked around the ghostly *Sinclair* for most of a morning, my feelings went back and forth between curiosity and anxiety. None of the doors were locked and there was no evidence that she'd been afire along more than half her length. I could only imagine what it had been like that savage dawn.

In the early months of the war, many ships were torpedoed off the East Coast, hugging the shoreline south to avoid the Gulf Stream northward current. Waterfront communities and especially Florida resort hotel owners refused to dim their lights, making silhouetted vessels, mostly tankers, easy targets. There was a six-mile neon stretch at Miami alone, where tanker murder was committed.

The crew began to report aboard and there was a frantic bustle to load stores and all manner of equipment, including ammunition. We worked fifteen-hour days. It became apparent that she had a small collection of maritime veterans but mostly greenies like myself.

I soon met the mates, the ship's officers. Chief Mate Evert Alanne was Finnish and had been sailing for forty years. Our second mate, the navigator, was in his thirties and had served aboard many tankers. His body was a mass of scar tissue from severe burns after being torpedoed. He did not go ashore the whole time I was on the *Annibal*. He did not want women to see his face, which had the texture of almond shells. I used him as a character model for "Chip Clewt" in *The Weirdo*, 1991. The third mate was white-haired and sixty something. He kept asking the one-legged radio operator, another torpedo casualty, to listen for stock market reports. He was said to be a millionaire and had come out of retirement to aid his country. Chief Mate Alanne selected me to be his lookout. I didn't realize how lucky I was.

The talk was of U-boats.

∽o∾

I received advice from the ship's machinist, another veteran: "If we have fire on the water, jump into the discharge stream." That was the big pipe outlet located on the hull above the waterline off the engine room. The strong flow of the discharge would buffer the burning oil or gas on the surface, allowing the swimmer to drop back into the wake of the ship. Yeah, okay.

Reality, for me, set in when I was down in Tank Three, starboard, just forward of the bridge, where the torpedo had hit. I was cleaning scale pockets, plain old rust, with wooden scoops—no risk of sparks to light hidden vapors—when I saw a small pile of charred human bones. The poor soul hadn't made it to the discharge stream. Later I dreamt about him burning alive.

Within the week, the *Sinclair*, now named *Annibal*—though the new name didn't appear on the stern so that sub captains couldn't identify her in case we were sunk—sailed from Baltimore for Hampton Roads, Virginia, at the foot of Chesapeake Bay. When identification was needed in port or at anchor, we had wooden name boards to hang on each wing of the bridge. We had a new master, Jonas Moe, another Finn.

The ships that had been destroyed thus far in the American theatre of war—East Coast, Gulf of Mexico, and Caribbean Sea—had been traveling alone. For a while, some had leap-frogged between ports in daylight runs of one hundred twenty miles, ducking into steel net-protected anchorages, or natural harbors, waiting out the night. Up to the end of April, eighty-two had been sunk from Nova Scotia to Key West; other sinkings had occurred in the Gulf of Mexico and Caribbean Sea. My uneasiness continued.

Great convoys, masses of ships escorted by naval vessels of all types, were the only answer. The first one sailed from New York in late August, 1942, headed for Guantanamo Bay, Cuba. From then until 1944, when the worst of the sub menace was finally licked, convoys were always underway somewhere around the world. Much earlier, they'd proved successful on TransAtlantic, Russian supply, and Mediterranean routes.

Eventually, convoys operated like local and express trains. Ships came out of ports to join the passing convoys like floating boxcars. The world had never seen anything like the intricate global movement of multinational cargo carriers. Likely, the world would never again see thousands of ships shepherded by hundreds of naval vessels. I was overwhelmed by the sheer size.

Word got out that once we reached Hampton Roads shipping waters, we'd anchor and wait for five or six other ships, then go out and join a major group headed south, riding outside the eastern edge of the Gulf Stream. Soon we steamed into the historic "Roads," waters George Washington knew.

So now, at long last, I was going to sea during a brutal U-boat war. I think I was typical of most young Americans of the time, one part of me wanting to go out and fight the Germans and Japanese; another part of me afraid I'd never come back. Naked fear.

At last we sailed, with four patrol craft pacing alongside, and two blimps dramatically overhead, armed with depth charges. Uneasiness and some of the fear began to vanish as we cleared the Virginia Capes, heading due east to rendezvous with the main group. For the next four hours I stood look-out either on the bow, up in the crow's nest, which I preferred, or on a bridge wing. I didn't need to be told to watch for a periscope wake. I stole glances at the escorts, with their blinking signal lamps and at the blimps, but most of the time I was sweeping the sea. The day was clear and cold, I remember.

A day later, on Chief Mate Alanne's afternoon four-to-eight watch when I shifted lookout from the starboard bridge wing up to the crow's nest, we were crossing on a southeasterly course the edge of the indigo blue Tropic Gulf Stream. It was littered with orange-colored seaweed and the treacherously beautiful Portuguese men-o-war, jelly-fish with poisonous tentacles that reached down forty to sixty feet. Their multi-colored gelatinous "sails" propelled them. I was awed by the colors. Over the next months I learned a lot about "the stream" from big-bellied Alanne. Originating in the Gulf of Mexico, it is the most remarkable of all ocean currents.

Just before sundown we spotted the main convoy—always an awesome sight, whether viewed from the ships or from the air. For TransAtlantic convoys there would be as many as sixty vessels with a ring of escorts, up to and including battleships if troopships were involved in the caravan. Groups of U-boats, "wolf-packs," were attacking in mid-Atlantic. Later, even aircraft carriers were added to escort duty. The masses of ships moved at a designated speed, attempting to keep position fore-and-aft, usually six hundred yards apart bow to stern and a thousand yards between columns.

Our unit of six ships fell in behind the 7.5-knot main group of twenty-two, while two of our escorts peeled off to return to Norfolk. The escorts that day included armed trawlers, a pair of old destroyers, and what appeared to be a large, armed yacht. What wasn't known aboard the *Annibal* was that the U-boats had been picking off ships even in the presence of escorts. Our defenses were still feeble.

In open sea, the bridge wings were lonely and the mates often left their usual positions by the helm to come out on the wings and chat. Alanne often did that, speaking softly in his Helsinki accent. Weather became "wedder." Having gone to sea as a boy on sailing vessels, Alanne knew ships, the stars, the winds, and the currents and he opened a treasure chest of sea stories once he discovered I was a serious student. Off-watch, I kept a notebook to jot down the stories.

His binoculars were always busy, even when he walked the bridge—through the pilot house doors to the opposite wing and back again. He'd spot something floating on the water and focus on the flotsam. A box, a huge tangle of seaweed, a cypress knee root out of the North Carolina swamps.

He'd learned the seabirds of the world and could imitate the loud, bugle-like call of the herring gull. He knew the storm petrels that danced over the surface with wings held high, flying determinedly far out over the oceans. He was familiar with the blue-faced boobies, frigate birds, and ospreys, pointing them out. He knew the stars intimately—Polaris, Arcturus, Regulus, Achenar, and Deneb Kaitos. He became my teacher, responsible for ten books about the sea and many short stories.

∽o∾

Fore and aft, and off each side were ships parading. Beyond them and ahead were the Naval escorts, some hull-down on the horizon. The spectacle provided a constant show for newcomers like myself and even the seasoned sailors who'd made trips in British convoys long before Pearl Harbor. No two ships were alike in appearance or performance. There were always a few that trailed smoke from their stacks, drawing the attention of both enemy sub lookouts and angry escort commanders. Then there were the laggards, falling behind in their columns, causing steering problems for following vessels, sometimes becoming U–boat targets.

At night, totally blacked-out, the ships had to steer on the prescribed courses, reducing or increasing the propeller turns to attempt to stay those six hundred yards apart, bow to stern. The mates eyes strained to catch the wake of the ship ahead, slowing down if too close. There were occasional collisions at night.

My third dawn, still jittery up in the crow's nest, sweeping around with the binoculars, I thought I saw a periscope in the middle of the lane between the *Annibal's* column and the column next door. I yelled, "Periscope, periscope off the starboard bow!" into the speaking tube. It took only a few seconds until Alanne's voice spiraled out of the tube. "Driftwood," he said calmly. He'd been at war since 1939.

After the watch was over, I apologized for the false report. He advised me to always immediately notify the bridge of whatever I spotted, no matter if it later turned out to be harmless flotsam.

Occasionally, we'd hear the echo of Navy depth charges, explosives dropped or hurled overboard by one or more of the escorts. The entire convoy would come to an alert though there was always the possibility of a false sonar contact on a U-boat. Unlike the British, the jittery U.S. Navy sub-hunters had little experience at this point. The first enemy submarine loss off the East Coast had occurred in April.

Over the course of World War II I rode six different ships, both merchant and Navy, as a cadet, an able-bodied seaman, a third mate and an ensign. Yet I was never bored watching the water. There was always something happening out there, birds or schools of fish or turtles or whales or other ships. *I could have sailed forever,* I thought. Writing and sailing would be my life.

We were bound for Curacao in the Dutch West Indies.

CURACAO

One morning Alanne talked to me about an area on the North Atlantic passage from New York to England. The Germans called it *das Todesloch,* the Death Hole. He'd sailed it several times. American and British sailors called it the Gorge or Abyss. It was in the absolute middle of the Atlantic where there was no air protection from either America or England.

The wolf-packs staged attacks against the convoys there, sometimes sinking six or eight ships during the course of a single night. He told me about a British liner transporting children to the safety of Canada. She was sunk and half a dozen children in nightclothes got onto a big life raft. The attacking sub skipper saw them in his spotlight and refused to rescue them. I eventually used the scene in *To Kill The Leopard*, 1993.

Usually, tankers, even when empty, were given inside positions in the convoys so that the U-boats would have a tougher time hitting them. Freighters were placed in the outside lanes and at the column ends, always vulnerable to attack.

Each ship, even ships of the same type, has its own personality. There is a difference, small or large, in how they respond to the helm, particularly older ships; and in how they respond to increased or decreased engine revolutions. Tankers, when fully loaded, take longer to stop than freighters. The liquid cargo is continually moving.

It took me a while to learn how to steer the *Annibal* and to be trusted entering or leaving port, listening to the commands of the harbor pilots. On the open sea, I stood two-hour "wheel watches" unless we were using the automatic pilot, which steered the ship on set courses. In convoy, the Navy demanded a seaman on the big helm at all times. I loved the "wheel watches," so much steel in my hands.

The *Annibal* plodded routinely along bearing south, keeping convoy "station" rather well night and day. At night, the compass face, hooded to contain the light on the blacked-out bridge, often had a mesmerizing effect. The soft click of its helm, the movement of the spear-shaped "cardinal points" on its card, all of it floating in liquid in a bowl of cast bronze—it could lull you into a doze after a busy day.

We were approaching the Spanish Main, the route of the old Galleons and the haunts of pirates. Now and then a native trading schooner would be sighted, seemingly unimpressed by the passing armada. They had the right of way but chose not to exercise it. My lifetime love affair with *Mar Caribe* had begun. As we steamed along, southing every hour, I had no idea that I'd sail her painted waters a lot of times, visit many of her islands, even live on one of them before the tour ships and great airports ruined them. I was being conditioned for *The Cay* and didn't know it.

As a kid, back in the days when geography was actually taught, I'd looked at the Bahama Islands, Cuba, Haiti, and Puerto Rico on maps, and now, here were the Bahamas, stirring the imagination with palm tree settings. I eventually became, between war and peace, an island junkie. Eight books have had the romantic, isolated island settings. I once went around the world island hopping.

I remember one night when Alanne told me that the reason he'd gone to sea as a mess boy on a tanker was his desire to sail warm waters. He'd been born in the quaint city of Espoo, not far from

Helsinki, where the winters were indeed long, dark, and cold. He named off islands I'd never heard of in the Java Sea, the Molucca Seas, the Banda and Arafura Seas. The exotic names alone pulsed with barefoot sailors, schooners, and white sand beaches. I really had a bad case of Robert Louis Stevenson and Paul Gauguin. I used Alanne's island memories in *A Sailor Returns,* 2001, augmented with research.

The convoy swept through Mona Passage, between the Dominican Republic and Puerto Rico, four freighters breaking away to proceed on to Guantanamo Bay where they would join a convoy bound for the Panama Canal and Pacific Ocean.

We sailed on almost due south toward Curacao.

In heavy weather, when the *Annibal* was fully loaded, seas lashed across the well decks and the catwalk traveler had to hang on to keep from being knocked about. During several hurricanes, I had my share of excitement on the two-by-six longitudinal boards. Once, I was knocked flat on the forward well deck and had to be rescued before I was washed overboard. Hurricanes have figured in four books, first in *The Cay.*

After the crossing from Mona Passage, I watched from the bridge as the pastel-colored, Rotterdam-style, gabled buildings of Curacao arose under the soft glow of the midnight moon. Ships had been torpedoed within sight of land when the moon was full. To the north, the processing flames of the Curacaosche Petroleum Maatschappij refineries blazed against the sky. The smell of gas and oil was heavy, floating like an unseen cloud above us.

The Dutch pilots, picked up from a small boat several miles at sea, were guiding each ship as we passed the famous swinging pedestrian bridge and entered St. Annabaai, then passed on into the Schottegat, the huge harbor, where Allied tankers were moored side-by-side for acres, waiting to be loaded and sent out to sea again.

I remember the anticipation, the thrill, of that first foreign port. Perhaps it was because I was still a "hayseed," raised in unexotic places, seldom ever hearing a foreign tongue, seeing street spelled "straat," wharf spelled "werf." I'd lived all my life in a country where most towns are less than a hundred-fifty years old. Curacao dated to the sixteenth century.

The wise writer collects these sights, smells, and sounds and stores them in memory, never knowing when they can be used in a piece of work.

∽o∽

I went ashore with the bosun's mate, a Texan, boss of the deckhands. Our primary mission that first late afternoon was drinking. We had survived the voyage, "so bottoms up." The crowded water taxi dropped us off at a dock in Punda, Willemstad's relatively small commercial area. Tankermen from everywhere thronged the streets, some so drunk their knees wouldn't operate.

What I'd first seen coming into St. Anna's Bay under the bright moon the night before last—red tile roofed, gabled buildings of pasteled saffron, green, pink orange, brown, red—two or three stories high were along Handelskade, then flowed eastward, structure by structure, large and small, in a soothing paintpot, though not exactly the same shades. A governor in 1817 had decreed that the island's buildings must be colored to off-set the glaring sun.

Tied up on the Waaigat, the inlet separating the businesses from residential Scharloo, were noisy and colorful schooners from Venezuela with fresh seafood, fruits, and vegetables. The island's desert soil did not yield very much food. Palm trees and plants were imported.

We went by the schooner market on the way to a bar that Bosun Jack Owens had frequented several times in earlier voyages. It faced De Ruyterkade across from the Central Market. The narrow swill joint was smoky and loud with jukebox music, and sailors were shoulder to shoulder. Jack had warned me not to come ashore in my cadet uniform to avoid derision. I wore khaki pants and a denim shirt, blending in.

Some tankermen had decided that this might be their last great drunk before being incinerated on the trip north, Bosun said. But everyone in combat zones on land, sea, or in the air had those thoughts. Writers or would-be writers should observe such social gatherings. Immediate departure is also a good idea when knives are pulled. We consumed a lot of rum that night. Fights broke out with little warning, but we avoided trouble. The only time I'd ever been a knife target was in New Orleans; the wielder a drunken Latino sailor.

I went ashore by myself the next afternoon and took a tour on an open air bus, not knowing that I'd later use Curacao as the initial setting of *The Cay*, the best piece of writing I could ever expect to do. The shaky old Chevy bus lurched and bounced around the rocky, arid countryside. Cacti and thorn bushes grew everywhere. Two more trips to Curacao and I got to know the island.

On the Schottegat, where the dozens of huge oil, gas, and diesel tanks sat like huge brown mushrooms on the shore, it was time to load the *Annibal* and have her ready for the convoy north. The chief mate was always in charge of loading, night or day, and Alanne stayed on the well decks until the operation was over, periodically taking samples as the cargo came aboard to insure quality. The 73,000-plus barrels of high octane gasoline were finally topped off. The individual steel tank hatches projected about three feet off the deck, with small, round breathing vents located in the center of them. The smell of the liquid dynamite was heavy in the tropic air. I was anxious to have it pumped out.

Before we departed, a drunken messman named Shorty, angry at the world in general, threw a lighted cigarette at a screened tank breathing vent. He could have blown up the *Annibal*. I used Shorty in *Rogue Wave*, a story about the sea, 1996.

So the convoy sailed, after five days in port, with many of the same ships that we'd joined off Norfolk, picking up an additional five or six, all loaded, all headed up the East Coast, some on to England to fuel Allied aircraft. The return route would carry us up the middle of the Gulf Stream until it began to swing eastward off Cape Hatteras. Destination Norfolk Naval Air Base.

When we'd safely reached a position roughly due east of Daytona Beach, Florida, the convoy blacked-out. There was a sudden red mass to the west, and the slam of an explosion. Having relieved the 12-to-4 wheel watch about ten minutes previously, my head wasn't entirely clear of sleep, but that condition lasted only seconds. The convoy was under attack. Alanne matter-of-factly said, "Just keep her steady," as Captain Moe came out of his sea cabin in pajamas.

Within minutes, the dull thuds of destroyer depth charges punched at the hull. At first light, one of the foreign tankers was missing. We sailed on, our aviation gas cargo intact.

I'd fallen in love with the old, creaky *Annibal,* as I'd fallen in love with the *Star* and *Daily News,* and would have been perfectly happy to remain aboard her until the end of the war, whenever that would be. Alanne, with that great bulging stomach, had become a sea-going father to me in many ways. Perhaps I was still seeking a real father, someone who would talk to me about other than the workingman. It mattered not that Alanne dwelt solely on the sea and ships to entertain me, to teach me. I think he enjoyed the student-professor relationship. The daily hours that I spent on watch with him never seemed dull. Perhaps I was the son he never had? Or did have? We didn't deal in personal matters.

We crossed the Gulf of Mexico several times, headed for the oil ports, and on one occasion ran into a hurricane with winds of 130 mph. Hurricanes are no problem for tankers. If light, you just load the tanks with sea water down to the plimsoll marks and plough on, waves breaking dramatically over the bow and well decks. The only inconvenience is not being able to cross the catwalk back to the dining saloon for fifteen or twenty hours. Wind drove the rain with such force that it stripped the paint off of us on that voyage.

I began my first novel while on the *Annibal*. Entitled *Big Red, Little Red,* it was about two sailors, both redheads, the smaller one influencing the larger one, leading to the downfall of both. They were ordinary seamen, a step above apprentice, on the ship and I could observe them daily. I thought of scenes while standing lookout watch either on the bridge or in the crow's nest. I'd work on the book off-watch in my bunk. The practice of taking characters from real life and using them as models started with that first amateurish book, which was never finished. I wrote fifty-odd pages, then ran out of ideas.

The Pacific Ocean, and primarily the refinery at Talara, Peru, was the next venue and included two trips with high-test aircraft gasoline for carriers operating thousands of miles away.

After steaming for almost a year and a half, the *Annibal* needed rest and a long stay in a repair yard, so the War Shipping Administration ordered us back to Baltimore. Usually, the deck and engine cadets were taken off at-sea training after a maximum six months. I'd avoided that unwanted termination one way or another. I had passed all of my correspondence extension quizzes, having trouble only with navigation and meteorology, but aided in both cases by Alanne.

Receiving stern orders to report back to King's Point upon our arrival in Baltimore, I sent off a letter from Panama saying my entire experience had been on a tanker. Shouldn't I be rounded out with freighter experience? I practically begged the training department and I was ordered to a venerable American Export ship, the *Exanthia,* then loading general army cargo in Brooklyn. She was headed for the United Kingdom. I said good-bye to Alanne with deep regret. I'd learned much on the *Annibal*.

With heavy tanks lashed down on the fore-and-after decks, the

Exanthia had light tanks and ammunition in her cavernous holds. In a sixty-ship convoy, we sailed for Cardiff, Wales, in support of the invasion forces that had landed in France in June. What we brought to Cardiff would have to be staged over to France as needed.

We'd been at sea eleven days and were nearing the British Isles when the tanker SS *Jacksonville,* riding in the next column to us and loaded with aviation gasoline, made a turn, together with four other ships breaking away to go to Loch Ewe, Scotland, and Belfast, Ireland.

I had the 12-to-4 lookout watch that early afternoon and felt the shock waves slam our ship as the *Jacksonville* exploded, hit by a torpedo near her bridge. She was a mass of flames that reached at least two hundred feet stem to stern. I watched as she burned. Out of a crew of seventy, only two survived. On that trip, two more convoy ships, both freighters, were lost to German submarines' last-ditch efforts to stop the millions of tons of supplies moving toward Europe. The main body of the convoy was still plodding on to the safety of the Irish Sea, though escorts were frantically searching for one or more U-boats. Doctrine was that the ships keep in columns, *keep moving,* swallow the losses of hulls and shipmates.

∽⊙∾

Returning to New York without a single mishap, I reluctantly boarded the train for King's Point, thinking they'd keep me on land for at least another year. Much to my surprise and delight I had an option. After a short license prep course, I could sit for the third mate's Coast Guard exam but wouldn't "graduate" from the four-year Academy. I'd receive a fancy diploma saying that I'd finished courses of the U.S. Merchant Marine Cadet Corps. I couldn't have asked for more. Dating back to high school, diplomas didn't impress me.

Predictably, I failed navigation at the first exam sitting, the math nemesis haunting me again. But passed it after hiring a tutor in Brooklyn, a retired sea captain. I considered this a miracle and, ironically, my first job after obtaining third mate "papers" was as acting second mate on a molasses tanker. The second mate is the navigation officer on most ships. I had no idea how I would get by if the master handed me a sextant.

I boarded my new ship, the SS *Castana*, in Philadelphia. An old "Hog Islander" tanker, she'd been built at the end of World War I at Hog Island, a swampy section of land which is now the Philadelphia Airport. The distinctive "Hogs" were noted for a lack of sheer, a straight bow, and a counter stern. They were slow and dumpy. The bridgehouse and engine were separated by a cargo hold. No other vessels looked like the antiquated Hogs. I'd never heard of a molasses-hauling ship and had no idea that the sticky cargo was being converted to alcohol at the Publicker Works in Philly.

Dinner had long been served by the time I boarded, and I immediately went to bed after being told that she'd sail in several hours. I wasn't needed on the fantail for departure, the second's customary station when the lines to shore are dropped. I'd noticed a bug spray smell in my stateroom but paid little attention to it. At approximately 11:30 there was a hard knock on the door and a voice shouted, "Time to wake up, mate." I had thirty minutes to get ready before I relieved the third mate. Turning on the bunk light, I saw that the entire bedspread was covered with cockroaches seeking warmth, most of them two inches long. Awakening once, I thought I'd felt something cross my face.

Hundreds were on the deck and I squashed many with my bare feet going for my clothes and shoes. Welcome to the "Hog." These were undoubtedly Cuban cockroaches, not Pennsylvania species. We were headed for Nuevitas, southeast of Havana, to load.

The slow *Castana* had a problem returning to Philadelphia in zero weather. Her steam heating system in the tanks refused to operate somewhere opposite the Georgia coast, and the further north we went after leaving the Gulf Stream, the more the molasses congealed. By the time we anchored in Delaware Bay, the cargo was frozen solid and had to be dug out with shovels. Thankfully, the cockroaches also froze to death.

I departed the *Castana* even before the stevedore shovelers began work.

☙○❧

One advantage, especially for writers, of sailing merchant ships is that you seldom know where the next ship will take you. The whole world can become a series of destinations and without realizing it you take a part of the new port with you, saving it for the possibility of a story sometime or another.

My next one was the C-2 freighter-type *Cape Avinof*. She was berthed in Wilmington, Delaware, having finished sea trials but otherwise a maiden. New cars have a certain pleasing smell, and the *Avinof*, not long from the builder's ways, had that fresh, clean odor about her when I boarded to serve as third mate. The cargo, to be loaded in Philadelphia, was tanks and guns and ammunition.

One *Avinof* memory occurred off quaint Shoeburyness, England, at the mouth of The Thames. Part of a five-ship group bound for Antwerp, we dropped anchor long enough to receive a British commando unit armed with high-powered rifles.

The Nazis had become so desperate that they were using underwater swimmers to attach explosives to our ships going up the Westerschelde River. Parts of Holland and Belgium were still occupied by German troops. If the Schelde could be plugged, supplies for the Allied armies pushing toward victory would be reduced. The commando sergeant said, "Antwerp is still under attack." So it was.

The Germans were launching V-1 and V-2 rockets toward the port. The V-1 was known to the British as a "doodle-bug," a "flying bomb" and a "buzz bomb." Twenty-five feet long with a 16-foot wingspan and powered by pulse jets, the V-1 carried a one-ton warhead and could travel about 250 miles at about 400 mph. The guidance system was faulty and the Germans fired them at general, not specific, target areas. Sounding like aerial burps on their descent, they were psychological weapons. In our time in Antwerp I saw four of them, gliding down and burping away, then exploding. It was useless to run.

The second one I saw had every chance of hitting the *Avinof* but, luckily for us, fell instead in the open after cargo hold of the British ship just ahead of us. About twenty Belgian stevedores were down in the hold. I was on our foredeck where cargo was also being worked. Body pieces showered over our foredeck as the corpses were flung high into the air. Blood and flesh fell on me. The chances of that hit were probably a million to one. V-1s were terrifying weapons.

The *Avinof* returned to New York, where it loaded and then sailed in convoy for the Mediterranean. We stopped first in Oran, North Africa, to discharge two huge "mystery" crates, then proceeded to Marseille, which was still smoking. The French port had been liberated but the damage of the bombing and fighting, especially on the waterfront, could be seen everywhere.

I went ashore the second night and found a candlelit bar on the waterfront. Bad cognac was available and I partook, noticing that two American GIs were practically terrorizing the premises. I stood far away from them. Then suddenly through the door came a French Senegalese officer, at least 6' 5" tall, splendid in his uniform, tribal marks cut into his black cheeks. He saw immediately what the GIs were doing and stepped between them, saying nothing to them; his mere presence enough to shut them up and ease them out into the night.

He became the character of Dumbele in *Walking Up a Rainbow,* 1986.

The European war ended like an exhausted wobbling tire gone flat. Admiral Doenitz, the same U-boat Doenitz of *To Kill the Leopard*, surrendered Germany while we were still at dockside in Marseille.

After six years of undersea warfare, convoys were no longer needed, and the *Avinof* sailed back alone through the Death Hole.

For several days, it seemed odd to go to the bridge without seeing ships pushing along on either side, ahead, and astern.

Returning to New York, I opened Navy orders to report to the USS *Draco* as an Ensign USNR. She was out in the Pacific. The Navy had begun to prepare for the invasion of Japan, which would require hundreds of freighters and tankers. Cargo officers were needed and I was fully qualified. The *Draco* was a well-worn Liberty hull.

BIKINI ATOLL

In mid-January, 1946, I was in Pearl Harbor awaiting orders to another ship. How the pre-computer Navy kept account of thousands of sailors was mind-boggling. Somehow, the Bureau of Naval Personnel in Arlington, Virginia, managed to know exactly where we were.

The war was over, of course, atom bombs having exploded over Hiroshima and Nagasaki, but I still didn't have enough Navy service points for release back to civilian life. I remember lacking ten or twelve. I wasn't in any particular hurry, anyway. The sea had me firmly in her bosom, and I was thinking about returning to the merchant marine once I did get out, combining ships and writing, endlessly traveling the world, maybe going to Java in person.

In the Officer's Club, the "O Club," at Pearl, I ran into a buddy from Portsmouth and we drank our lunch, not uncommon for junior officers in 1946. Staggering out, in brilliant sunshine and soft air, I noticed a sign I hadn't seen coming in: *Officer Volunteers Wanted for Operation Crossroads.* It was the Navy's plea to sailors to stay in a while longer. The Navy had a huge problem that year: Personnel were leaving pell-mell and there were critical jobs to be filled, especially in technical areas. Aircraft were land-bound in the Pacific because of a lack of mechanics. Some ships were operating with one-third their normal crews.

I gazed at the sign for a hazy moment or two. I knew what Operation Crossroads was all about. A pair of atom bombs were going to be exploded at Bikini Atoll, in the North Pacific, 2,200 miles from Hawaii. Almost a hundred target ships would be anchored in the lagoon to await the nuclear blasts—one from the air, the other underwater.

My friend wasn't interested. A girl was waiting for him in Portsmouth and he'd have enough points in less than a month to say good-bye. He wasn't fond of the Navy, anyway. He wanted to go back to college. I had no such lofty plans, no girlfriends waiting anywhere. *Perhaps I could write a book about the bomb blasts.*

I weaved to the personnel offices and found the right desk, offering my services. The wheels turned quickly. I hitchhiked aboard a small carrier, a "jeep." I think it was the *Siboney*. I was off-loaded at Kwajelein Atoll, which hadn't changed much since 1944 when it suffered the most intense artillery bombardment of World War II. It was a shambles; rusting Japanese guns, vehicles, and human skeletons were still there.

The C-46 transport plane that was to take several of us to bomb-battered Eniwetok Atoll had been trying to get off the ground for a week without success. Five tries failed due to engine trouble. Finally, the pilot said, half-looped, "Well, we're gonna go. I'm gonna take the damn door off so if we splash, you guys can just walk out." He was going to fly at five hundred feet over the blue sea. The old C-46 was molasses slow, so we'd just float in and settle into the warm water. He'd put three rubber rafts aboard. I remember getting drunk that night in the Kwajelein O Club, laughing a lot at the whole silly idea of flying with an open door.

From Eniwetok I hitchhiked again to Bikini Atoll on a Coast Guard buoy-tender and couldn't believe the peace and beauty of the lagoon and main island. Bikini hadn't really been disturbed by the war, though it was occupied by the Japanese for a while. There were some outriggers skimming around the blue-green waters, and ashore were thousands of palm trees. Fish jumped, sea birds winged by. Until I saw the Seychelles much later, Bikini was the single most beautiful island I'd ever seen.

Reporting to the USS *Sumner*, a geodetic survey ship anchored in the lagoon, I couldn't believe that we were going to "nuke" this paradise. The Sumner, having arrived a few days earlier, was an old submarine tender converted to survey work. She had a bow like the bill of a storm petrel. With printing presses aboard, she had been the chartmaker for the invasion forces, involved in combat, an illustrious ship.

An old shoe of a vessel, with teakwood decks and mahogany interiors, it was like a big, plush yacht inside, designed to comfort submariners while their craft underwent repairs. Our job at Bikini was to destroy sea bottom coral heads in the target areas and establish instrumentation and navigational towers ashore for all sorts of measurement devices and cameras. We would also plant buoys and rechart the lagoon.

The crusty executive officer, a former chief bosun's mate, asked about experience. Handling cargo, I said, in the merchant marine and on the *Draco*. "You'll command a drag boat. Welcome aboard." What was a drag boat?

There were four drag teams, each operating a forty-foot diesel-powered boat in search of dangerous coral heads, some extending forty or fifty feet up from the bottom. After towed drags located the coral, divers were sent down to place dynamite charges.

The natives had not been told about Operation Crossroads, yet the *Sumner* drag teams were already busily destroying the tough coral heads. Yellowish explosions ripped the peace and quiet, discoloring the water and leaving hundreds of dead fish floating on the surface. No one had told the natives about atom bombs, either. They hadn't heard of Hiroshima.

On the third or fourth morning I had officer-of-the-deck duties, an outrigger tied up to our float. A native, the only one who could speak a little English I later learned, asked what we were doing there. I gave him a stupid ensign answer: "I don't know." He pressed me and I said, "It's a military secret." Most of the world knew about Operation Crossroads and it was only "secret" at Bikini Atoll. I lived with those and other lies for the next forty-eight years until I wrote *The Bomb,* 1995.

As the conquerors of Japan, the USA owned Bikini Atoll. We could do what we pleased, and we chose to explode the world's fourth and fifth atom bombs here in a few months, whether or not the 160-odd people who lived on the island, and truthfully owned it, agreed or not. I was deeply troubled by what we were doing.

Navy brass and some atomic scientists said they wanted to know if the ships would survive the cataclysmic force of nuclear explosions. Knowing as little as we did about Hiroshima and Nagasaki, it still seemed to most of us on the *Sumner* that the question had already been answered in Japan. There was constant debate in the officer's mess.

Animals would take the place of human crews on the clustered target ships. Goats would be tethered on the open decks; guinea pigs and five thousand rats would be inside the ships, along with cancer-prone white mice. Some of the goats and pigs would be shaved and smeared with anti-flash compounds. Goats and pigs have skin similar to humans. All would be exposed to radiation. I could only shake my head.

Around the wardroom table for meals, I can't remember anyone who favored what we were doing. We guessed more than knew what was going to happen to King Juda's gentle people and to their homeland. They might not be able to ever live there again. It was possible the white sands might be poisoned for a thousand years; the palm tree roots would suck the poison. It would be a modern "Trail of Tears," the Cherokee Indian tragedy of the 1800s.

The first American outsider to come aboard was a scientist from the National Museum, part of the Smithsonian. He'd come to do "before and after" studies: take three samples of all the wildlife and plants, then two years after the explosions come back and make comparisons. He was the first of many scientists to visit the atoll before Able Day on July 1.

He was given a stateroom in Officer's Country two doors from mine. Though the *Sumner* was air-conditioned, a stench soon crept from his quarters. He went ashore every morning and came back in late afternoon with burlap bags full of dead fish of all varieties and birds he'd shot down. He stayed up late tagging them prior to freezing.

Engaging him in conversation, I saw that he was excited about the experiments. Samples weren't available from Hiroshima or Nagasaki, human or animal. He was quiet and noncommittal when it came to the plight of the Bikini natives. Did he care? Apparently not.

Most afternoons, a recreation party would be sent ashore with an ample supply of beer, there to play softball or horseshoes. The first time I rode a landing craft to the beach I was approached by a young man I thought to be around sixteen. He spoke no English and I spoke no Marshallese, his language. But he had a smile like the newly-risen tropic sun. He was Sorry Rinamu of *The Bomb,* 1995. He spelled his name in the sand and I did the same.

Using a sort of sign language, he offered to show me around the island. I readily accepted and followed him, walking the beach sands. I tried to observe everything on that first visit ashore and on other visits.

Behind the single street of crushed pink coral, there were twenty-six dwellings spread evenly along the central part of the island. The eleven families lived outdoors; their cool, high-peaked pandanus houses, with movable thatch walls, were mainly for sleeping. In windy and rainy seasons, the decorated window matting could be unrolled.

I was stunned by the simplicity and visual goodness of their lives although they were entirely impoverished. As we passed, they smiled and waved, not knowing what we much-envied Americans were about to do to them. As I said good-bye to the boy that day, my lies of the past week hurt more than ever. I was determined to return to the beach soon, look him up, and give him a gift; apologize, as if he could understand.

Sorry Rinamu was barely five feet. His head was crowned with black curly hair. His skin was dark brown. He looked a lot like his late father, who had been short and stocky, a man of quiet strength. All sinew, no fat. How Badina died out on the water, no one knew. The mystery troubled Sorry. [1]

On February 26, 1946, a PBY Catalina amphibious aircraft land-ed near the *Sumner* carrying the military governor of the Marshall Islands, Commodore Ben Wyatt. Commodore is one rank beneath rear admiral. A squat little man, former naval aviator, his mission was to inform the natives of Bikini that their homeland was going to be atomized. We provided a boat to land Wyatt, along with a staff mem-ber and an interpreter, on the beach. Ashore, church services were being held as was customary on Sunday mornings. Their Bibles had been translated to Marshallese.

Naval intelligence had told the commodore that the atoll people were very religious, and he immediately seized on their worship of God to persuade them to leave their homes for this great "scientific experiment." He talked about Moses and the children of Israel being led into the promised land. He said Bikini had been selected as the best site to test these weapons and would they please the Lord and agree to leave home for several years. He was lying to them.

He did not tell them that President Truman had already approved their lagoon for Crossroads. Nor did he tell them that they'd be marched away at gunpoint if they refused to leave. He did not offer money to them for giving up their ancestral homeland, and he lied when he said they could return in two years. Two, perhaps three bombs, then peace and quiet would return to the lagoon, he promised.

King Juda and the entire population sat in the sand under the palm trees, not far from their church, nodding solemnly. Then the clans voted nine to two to turn over the atoll to the powerful men from the east. These same Americans had liberated them from the

(1) *The Bomb*

Japanese. They had ships and guns and aircraft; the Bikinians grew coconuts and speared fish. They had no weapons. Fear was the reason they would leave, the only reason.

Back aboard the *Sumner,* Commodore Wyatt sat in the wardroom sipping iced tea and describing at length his victorious meeting with King Juda and the natives. Vastly pleased with himself, he'd accomplished his mission in little more than an hour.

Most of us listened that afternoon with revulsion and sadness. I wondered if he'd looked around the village, ducked his head inside a hut, sniffed their individual cookhouses, visited their church, walked around their graveyard, picked up a child? Did he see or think about the culture we were about to destroy?

Realistically, Wyatt was just doing what he was told to do. Orders!

On March 7, less than a month after the commodore first visited, a landing ship tank (LST), an ugly boxy carrier of troops and tanks, backed away from the beach with the entire population of Bikini aboard, along with all their worldly possessions—their outriggers, their pandanus (sleep and hut matting), and their pigs, dogs, and chickens. For hundreds of years the people had slept contentedly on their mats in the soft sand, now they'd live in wooden huts with wooden floors.

Their possessions were indeed few. The richest man on the atoll owned a hand-powered sewing machine. The Rinamu family owned a wooden chest of drawers and an axe. Their true wealth had been in coconuts. I tried to record what was happening in *The Bomb.*

As the LST passed near the *Sumner,* the people were singing a hymn and looking back toward their island. Sorry Rinamu was aboard, of course. They were bound for Rongerik, a miserable, uninhabited atoll 120 miles away. I remember their voices, their faces. There weren't many dry eyes, mine included, on our ship—and most of us were hardened combat veterans.

A day or two after the removal of the islanders, I went ashore and walked around what had been the village area. I remember sitting down in the sand and thinking about all that had happened in little more than a month and what would happen here in a few more months.

I remember finding a soiled homemade rag doll sitting upright against a dwelling, obviously the possession of a little girl who left it behind on purpose, a part of her to remain at home to watch over the land. In the novel it belongs to Lokileni, Sorry Rinamu's sister.

On June 30, the great mass of target ships in the lagoon—aircraft carriers *Saratoga* and *Independence,* battleships *Nevada, Pennsylvania, New York, Arkansas,* all kinds of fighting ships, almost a hundred of them—were abandoned. Only the animals remained aboard. The next morning, before nine o'clock, Able Bomb was dropped, exploding at five hundred feet. Most of the animals died. A month later, Baker Bomb blew up beneath the blue-green waters.

Operation Crossroads was a deadly and costly farce, providing little new information. Atom bombs could destroy ships, something fourth graders probably knew.

Atom bombs could destroy cities, men, women, and children, as the Japanese had learned. Some of the sailors who were ordered aboard the target ships to cleanse them of radiation, washing them down while in their tennies, later discovered what leukemia was all about.

I have a still picture to remind me what Operation Crossroads was all about: A radiated goat in a hospital bed being transfused after the Able blast. The look of bewilderment in its eyes cuts to the soul. *The Bomb* was a book I had to write, after long thought.

In 1995, for the fiftieth anniversary of Operation Crossroads I participated in two TV documentaries—one for French Canal, the other for the A & E History Channel, filmed by Dusmar Multimedia of Vancouver, Canada. A Dusmar camera sweep on Kili Island revealed a graveyard headstone bearing the name of Sorry Rinamu.

A NEW LIFE

Tests at Bikini over, the *Sumner* anchored in San Francisco Bay awaiting orders. Old as the ship was, a scrapyard was obviously at the end of her next voyage. She'd served admirably for more than a quarter of a century. Good ships often have sad deaths.

I met a sophisticated, dark-haired San Francisco girl on a blind date and enjoyed the nights ashore until we sailed for Norfolk for decommissioning and the cutting torch. After three intense weeks I was certain I was in love so I proposed marriage. Three weeks isn't enough time to decide on a new brand of toothpaste most of the time, much less marriage. But both Gwen Goodwin and I made the decision for nuptials somewhere on the East Coast in a few months. We later agreed it was a mistake.

By now I had plenty of points and ended my active duty with the Navy. I stayed several weeks in Florida with my parents, and then took a train to New York and went to Rockefeller Plaza, home of NBC. Congress had passed legislation during the war that provided guaranteed employment by the last company involved with the returning veteran. NBC was mine, as a sports writer, although Bill Stern was no longer there. But it was up to them to offer a job, naturally at a higher wage.

The employment director had obviously sat out the war at the RCA building and didn't seem too happy to have strangers showing up to claim labor rights. He said, "Many things have changed since you've been gone. You'll have to go to a six-week indoctrination course before we hire you back." Indoctrination for what? I was turned off immediately, the rebel and my father rising in me.

I never went back to the employment offices of NBC. Indoctrination, after four years of war, was not my idea of rejoining the world at peace. I hired on as the sports editor of the Bluefield, West Virginia, *Sunset News,* at twenty-five dollars a week, losing at least a hundred weekly. Though it didn't occur to me at the time, there was more of my father in me than I thought. God, he could be prickly and stubborn.

The coal fields in the Virginia mountains were not all that appealing after roaming halfway around the globe during the war. I'd made a major mistake. I missed going places and seeing things. Not much happened in the little town and sports were limited to the high school. Newly married in Bluefield and settling into that life was a challenge in a number of the usual ways. Just living intimately around the clock with someone else was a change in itself. My West Coast, uptown bride was accustomed to white rugs and I offered a one-room shack and a coal-burning stove for heating and cooking. Bluefield was a shock to her. Storms were ahead.

I had told Gwen that I wanted to be a freelance writer, a novelist, while dating in San Francisco and not too long after she got off the train prior to vows. That might mean insecurity and frustration on her part. I'm not sure she listened or took much stock in such a precarious goal. She wasn't much of a reader and preferred an orderly, no-dog, spotless, white rug existence, and considerable money. I don't think writers make very good husbands or wives. The divorce rate tends to be high.

Meanwhile, I took on sportscasting nightly at radio station WHIS for an extra ten dollars a week, Gillette Razors sponsoring.

But I quit both WHIS and the *Sunset News* in less than a year, my father chuckling. I was following his footsteps.

I've never been able to figure out why I suddenly decided to become a playwright and joined the American Theatre Wing in New York. A playwright? *Really?* I liked to see plays, but write them? Tuition was under the GI Bill of Rights and I soon found myself in drama school, of all places, living in an apartment on Riverside Drive at 116th Street, the Hudson lapping nine floors below. Thinking of myself as Tennessee Williams, then the prince of Broadway, was simply stupid.

Gwen got a job as a secretary. From day one, she hated New York, saying it lacked the charm of San Francisco. She missed the cable cars, even the fogs. I couldn't argue. Trouble was ahead.

Columbia University was just up the street and I enrolled for a night course by the eminent short story writer Martha Foley. Rejections arrived as I batted out bad work, unable to understand the character ingredients demanded in this genre. What arrogance it took to send a story to *The New Yorker* and others. Over the next few years of fury and frustration I must have been rejected two hundred times. I was not easy to live with. I wrote the Statesville short stories that Dr. Anderson had provided: *The Madstone, The Man with No Ears, The Hanging Sheriff.* I wrote *Tom Dooley.*

I soon wisely gave up trying to be a playwright. I was hired to be Assistant Director of Public Relations at New York University's Greenwich Village campus. Only then did I sell something. *Look Magazine* bought an article about a wonderful new thing called television about the time our first son, Mark, was born. He was destined to become my fishing pal.

One early morning when he was asleep in his crib, I looked down at him and saw a big black splotch of soot on his cheek, quite an ordinary happening in New York City. Time to go! I was still too much the Carolina fresh-air country person to endure oily visits through the open window. Time to find another job.

I didn't consider for a moment that I was duplicating my father in his almost endless performance of quitting. In my case, I didn't punch a boss and wasn't leaving my family behind. Next stop: Cocoa, Florida, on the Banana River, as correspondent for the *Orlando Sentinel-Star*, a newspaper that had a good reputation.

Not far away was Patrick Air Force Base and near it was a huge area of sandy palmetto-covered land, near the ocean, to be known initially as the Joint Long Range Proving Ground—the first concentrated space effort of the U.S. government. My job was to cover it and also act as a stringer for the Associated Press. At last, after several years of fumbling around, trying desperately to find myself, this might be exciting, a learning experience of the type that I found useful, like going to sea. Finally, I was writing again, and being paid for it. No rejections.

At Antwerp, blood-splattered, I'd seen firsthand the nature of rocket power in the V-1 and V-2 weapons developed at Pennemunde. Now I saw two captured V-2s sitting in a hangar at Patrick AFB. They had been modified and would soon be launched as the first military rockets to go skyward from the USA, an entry into the Space Age.

A thick concrete pad was laid in a desolate section, well away from the air base and the nearest scattering of houses. Then a trench was dug about fifty yards from the pad, hopefully providing an observation sanctuary from Bumper 8, where the missile was aimed straight up into the sky. Experts, including some Nazi scientists originally from Pennemunde and some reporters such as myself, would occupy the trench along with a few radio announcers. Also in the trench were motion picture cameras. TV hadn't been developed fully.

The problem was that no one knew exactly how this modified missile with ten tons of fuel aboard would perform. Would it go as planned or would it fall over and blow everyone within a quarter mile into hamburger meat? There was some anxiety among the sweating observers. I confess I was rather tight-lipped, remembering Antwerp.

On top of Bumper 8 was a seven hundred pound WAC Corporal missile developed for scientific, not military, use. At a prescribed altitude, the V-2 would "bump off" the Corporal and it would travel miles on up, hence the rather silly sounding name.

I'd been told that Canaveral would become the USA launch center for exploration of space and here I was, Mother Luck shining on me again, to be present at the making of history and a new language, "rocket speak." Part of my story follows:

Fueling finished at 8:27 A.M.
The countdown at X minus 22 minutes.
Two red flares to cross the sky at X minus three minutes.
Control Center said, "Hold at X minus two minutes."
The count starts again.
9:22, weather begins to close. Another hold.
9:26, two more red flares cross the sky.
9:27, Control Center said, "X minus one minute." Finally, "X minus zero."

There was a red flash at the pad. Dust puffed up and there was a hollow, rolling clap of thunder, as flames and smoke gushed from its bottom. Moving slowly, the slender steel tube seemed to hover around 100 feet and breaths in the trench were sucked in. Then, like the rocket it was, Bumper rose into the scattered clouds and dove through a hole about a mile up. Cheers went up from the trench. Traveling at 2700 mph, the V-2 "bumped off" the WAC Corporal after 83 seconds, eight and a half miles above the earth. At 160 seconds, the V-2 was destroyed out over the ocean . . .

This was pioneer stuff—*first USA military rocket*—an event that should be in history books, as if history is taught anymore except on the History Channel. Baby Boomer professors can be blamed. History is old-fashioned. No wonder students know little of our past. I was so lucky.

Almost a half century later—with space adventures routine and the moon walked upon, and stations gliding around earth becoming ordinary, and even talk of settling Mars perhaps—I think back to Bumpers 7 and 8 whenever I see a launch. Had I been a clerk at the Bank of Florida I never would have been in that trench. Then came heartbreaking *Mercury, Challenger* and *Columbia*.

In early spring 1950 I'd joined a Florida naval reserve unit to take advantage of "O Club" ten cent martinis and twenty-five cent chicken dinners. Mr. Truman more or less declared war against North Korea in June and I had orders assigning me to the cruiser USS *Newport News*. Someone in naval officer personnel discovered I'd worked on five newspapers. Suddenly there was a switch and orders were cut for me to report to the Pentagon and man a chair on the Navy Press Desk, with duties of writing press releases and providing information to the military reporters covering the new war. Another adventure.

The desks were across the hallway from the spacious Department of Defense Information Office on the second floor of that baffling building near the Potomac. Reporters from the *Washington Post, Washington Star, New York Times,* and other major newspapers and wire services walked back and forth to query the Army, Navy and Air Force news contingents on any number of issues, some uncomfortable. The newspapermen covering the Pentagon were usually understanding and so long as we tried to tell the truth, checking and back-checking "the brass," relations were good.

Mindful that I had a family that needed tending, daughter Wendy a new addition, I still wrote as much as I could during maddening off-hours from the Pentagon, sometimes on weekends, sometimes at night in the kitchen while others slept. I was tightly wound. We needed a car and the quickest way to get one was by magazine freelancing.

Every third weekend I had Saturday or Sunday duty in the Office of Information, alone there to take any calls for the combined services. The Pentagon on weekends tends to be spooky. On occasion, I'd be very busy if there was a breaking story from Korea. Most of the time the phones were quiet and I could either read a book or "rob the files." I did the latter.

The Army, Air Force, and Navy all had a cabinet where the week's press releases were stored, and I thumbed through them for article ideas. It was amazing what nuggets were in the files, all unclassified materials that the services hoped to get into print somehow. The Bureau of Ships might have an announcement about the development of a new type of propulsion that had civilian applications. I'd fatten the information by phone on Monday, then write it Tuesday night and sell it within a couple of weeks to a boating magazine.

My bible was a thick book titled *Writer's Market,* a listing of book and magazine publishers and addresses and names of editors, a reliable reference for newcomers to the wonderful world of words. I used another book of specific trade magazines. My targets were limited strictly to those who paid on acceptance. Looking back at the scrapbook of that feverish era, I see *Popular Mechanics, The New York Times Magazine, The Christian Science Monitor, Ships and Sailing, Men, Male,* and *Stag,* among others. *Popular Mechanics* was at the high end of pay; weekly *Grit* at the low at ten dollars. One can't afford to be choosy when climbing this particular ladder in search of money. Pride becomes a shrug. *Saga, Bluebook, Eye,* and others that no longer exist were markets.

I paid cash for the Nash Rambler and learned a lot about things that I really didn't care about. Beyond the fast money, the typewriter was kept busy, always a prerequisite for any professional writer.

A *New York Times* writer, Stacy Jones, wandered across the hall one morning, sat on the edge of my desk with a cup of coffee, saying, "I have a contract with E. P. Dutton to do a book on Admiral "Pete" Mitscher and I don't think I can do it." He'd been in the Army in World War II and knew nothing about the Navy. "I haven't even written a word. You interested?" We'd chatted now and then over a three-month period, newspaper talk mainly. He, too, had started out as a cub reporter. "Dutton advanced me five hundred dollars. The agent took fifty. I spent the rest."

Admiral Marc "Pete" Mitscher had led the fast carrier task forces across the Pacific with Admiral "Bull" Halsey during World War II. Mitscher had learned to fly not long after the Wright brothers' historic flight. Most of all he was a leader and his pilots worshiped him. I knew that much about him.

I got the idea. Jones would turn over the contract to me and walk away with $450 profit. I'm sure Dutton was attracted to him because of his *New York Times* bylines. Had I approached them, they likely would have said no thanks. I said, "Sure, I'd like to take a shot at it." A book? Why not?

It was all so casual that I almost forgot that a BOOK, a first book, might be ahead, every writer's dream. It was pinching myself time. At last, it was time to scream and shout.

"The agent can get the contract changed," Jones said.

On the morning of December 5, 1950, I was on duty when a dispatch came through from the Far East Naval Command. An ensign named Jesse Leroy Brown had been shot down over North Korea. I think I first read about Jesse Brown when I was a reporter for the Orlando paper. There had been an Associated Press story out of Jacksonville saying that he'd broken a "color barrier" to become the Navy's first black pilot. I recalled a picture of him in *Life Magazine*.

I remember the AP story saying he was a sharecropper's son. Knowing the Navy, with its tendency at the time to assign all black personnel to galleys as cooks and food servers, or to clean officer's staterooms, I wondered how he'd done it. How painful his struggle must have been, one young black man swimming upstream in a river of white pilot hopefuls and their often biased instructors. I wrote the press release about his death. There had to be a book in him, I thought. I put him in my "future file," but thinking that a black writer should undertake his story.

In January 1951, I began work on the biography of Admiral Mitscher, interviewing every source I could find who'd served with him from Annapolis until he died in 1946. The research alone was formidable because he was extraordinarily taciturn and left behind very few papers. He'd seldom talked about himself to reporters during the war or before. In some ways, he was a mystery man. I often worked on the book at nights and on weekends, neglecting my family to an extent. I flew on Navy aircraft to visit anyone who'd been close to Pete Mitscher. I found myself talking to World War II naval giants such as Bull Halsey.

Finishing the job in late fall, I impatiently awaited word from Dutton and received it Christmas Eve afternoon, 1951. I was decorating the Christmas tree in our northern Virginia house when the postman brought the letter of rejection. I almost fell off the ladder when Gwen passed it up. Devastated, I thought I'd written a good book but the editor disagreed and further asked that the five hundred dollar advance be returned. *Merry Christmas!*

By New Year's Day I'd gotten over the shock and outrage and read the manuscript word-for-word several times and finally agreed with Dutton that I'd turned in lesser work. I vowed to spend the next months on a re-write, adding more research, closing all the holes. The Dutton editor hadn't been much help in pointing out flaws but, thankfully, it was all a learning experience. W. W. Norton bought the heavily revised book for an advance of five hundred dollars and it was published in early fall 1954. Dutton had done me a great favor in rejecting it. I'd been obsessed by failure. The *New York Times* said, "A first-class biography . . ." The *New Yorker* said, "A fully-defined portrait of the scrappy, wizened man . . . " All the reviews were excellent.

I put in almost three years on the Navy press desk, continuing to freelance articles as well as sell a few short stories. It was interesting work, thumbing the pulse of a losing political war, surrounded by congenial people but really tired of that monster building, feeling like a motherless ant whenever I entered.

I began a quiet campaign to move my body back down to the warm, carefree Caribbean and in 1953 succeeded. With Mark, Wendy, and Gwen, I headed for Puerto Rico. Haiti, Grenada, Barbados, Carricou, Trinidad, St. Thomas, St. Croix, and St. John were also eventually added to my portfolio of islands leading to the flavors and rhythms of *The Cay*, 1969; *Monocolo*, 1989; *Timothy of the Cay*, 1993; and *A Torrent of Blood in Beautiful St. Thomas*, 2003.

THE FLICKS

Luck, for me, has usually been situational. Seldom blind. I've had both kinds, of course. Gambling—cards, dice, slots, horses—has never been rewarding and I've never been a risk-taker except on work. Months have been spent on short stories and novels that haven't been accepted, usual for almost any writer except for a Tom Clancy or John Grisham.

A copy of *The Magnificent Mitscher* tucked under my arm, I walked over to the Caribe Hilton Hotel and asked the desk clerk where I could find William Perlberg, the producer of *The Proud and Profane* starring William Holden and Deborah Kerr, then filming in Puerto Rico and St. Thomas. I'd started movie-going when I was six or seven in Statesville.

The clerk replied, "He's in the coffee shop," and pointed me in the right direction.

He was having breakfast as I introduced myself and said I wanted to give him a copy of my new book.

He said, "Sit down. I've had writers leave copies of their books on my toilet lids. I'm always interested in writers." We talked for a long while and eventually he offered me a job.

Walking under the famed arched gate of Paramount Pictures in the fall of 1954, I should have felt heaven-borne. As a teenager in Virginia I'd gone to Cradock's Afton Theater every time a movie changed. I had free passes from the *Daily News* to every moviehouse in Washington. I never missed a showing on the afterdecks of the *Draco* and *Sumner.* I should have been soaring. Why weren't my feet off the ground as I sought out Perlberg-Seaton Productions?

I don't know why but I remember they weren't. Maybe it was awe? Maybe I felt I wouldn't belong? Maybe I felt I wouldn't last? Just writer's insecurity, as Gwen had often pointed out. To an extent, I was worldly enough by then but likely not prepared for Hollywood. And I wanted to write books, not make movies. I was soon to serve legendary Clark Gable, Henry Fonda, Fred Astaire, Debbie Reynolds, Steve McQueen and others.

Make-believe was everywhere behind the office buildings lining Melrose Avenue in the heart of old-time cinema manufacturing. RKO Studios was just up the street and Columbia Pictures was about six blocks away. There were other smaller lots within walking distance. The corner of Hollywood Boulevard and Vine Street, a crossing known throughout the world, was within a longer walk. I was in a different storyland.

Walking the alleyways between the sound stages this noon hour were actresses and actors, some famous, in their makeup and emoting garbs. Just visiting this place of good and bad dreams was a rare treat for most people. There were no studio tours at the time. You walked under the arch either for business or by invitation.

Perlberg and Seaton were independent filmmakers, a rather new breed, financed by the studio and releasing through its distribution system. My starting weekly paycheck of $250, a breathtaking sum, the most money I'd ever made in my life, would come from Paramount, but I was Perlsea company's exclusive employee, hired as a press agent to exploit their films and none other.

Perlberg had become a producer after working as a talent agent and executive at Columbia. His thirty-eight credits on the screen included such distinguished films as *The Miracle on 34th Street* and

James Michener's *The Bridges of Toko-ri,* starring William Holden and Grace Kelly. Now "late-lates" or videos recommended for young eyes. Though rough and tough in business dealings, Perlberg had a keen sense of right and wrong in supervising the making of pictures. He knew good writing, good editing, good music, good acting.

George Seaton had had a stage and radio background before joining the MGM writing staff. He was radio's first Lone Ranger, pounding his chest with half coconut shells to imitate hooves. He was equally good with comedy or drama. An Academy Award winner for writing *The Country Girl,* with Grace Kelly and Bing Crosby, he was president of the Academy of Motion Picture Arts and Sciences, speaking on Oscar night, when I joined the team. As a writer-director he was among the best in town. Working with them was another chance to learn; my non-collegiate education would expand.

I could have been toiling in West Virginia for forty dollars a week. Now I'd be traveling first class with Perlberg-Seaton. They'd never made a B picture; their stars were box-office caliber and their films made money, the final compliment in "Tinsel-town."

Press agents, also known as publicists and "flacks" and other demeaning descriptions, work at an ignoble profession. The "spin-doctors" of Washington politics are actually press agents, grown men and women digging in mud. Movie press agents, dignifying themselves as publicists, come in several basic categories: those who write all manner of exploitation paragraphs for feeding to media; those who work gossip phones "planting" items; those who do both in "holding interview hands" of stars, directors, producers, company execs. There are all sorts of variations in the business of flackery. I soon learned them at a time when television was only a few years old, in black and white; when Internet could be a tennis term.

One morning, out of nowhere, Perlberg said, "I want you to go to Washington." He'd heard a true story about a Navy lieutenant who was put ashore in Inchon Harbor while it was still occupied by North Korean communists during that bloody war. His intelligence mission was to scout the enemy positions and then provide a light in a lighthouse to guide General MacArthur's invasion forces. To capture the lighthouse, he recruited teenagers from a school, as well as the school marm. Having been a gob, Perlberg was usually receptive to Navy stories. This one sounded pretty good: intelligence mission, armed children, school marm, a nice bag of intrigue.

I flew to Washington to try and track down the lieutenant, pry intelligence records loose, and see if the Navy would cooperate in making the film. I had Pentagon contacts. It occurred to me that perhaps that was one reason they'd offered me a job. I performed all my chores for Perlsea and then decided to take advantage of the trip for some research of my own.

Long before this well-paid movie thing, which was proving to be fun, I'd planned a book on the merchant marine battles with submarines in coastal waters. I knew about it; I'd been there on the *Annibal*. What burned me was that few people gave credit to the brave merchant seamen killed within sight of our beaches. I even had a title, *Fire on the Beaches*.

I spent some time with Navy documents and officials and then went over to the Coast Guard, where I knew the bulk of ship sinking records were stored, to research *Fire on the Beaches*, 1958. More than ten years had passed and, unlike the Navy, there weren't any classified materials to deal with, just personal accounts of torpedoings and what had happened to the hundreds of both foreign and USA flagged vessels.

The third or fourth morning, I came across a translated account of a Dutch ship that sailed from Curacao bound for the Panama Canal. She was hit after the sun had gone down the next day in a period of light known as "submarine or torpedo light." It occurs in the evening after sundown and before sunrise. The hulls of the subs were painted gray, matching the light, and could not be detected from the crow's nest or the bridge wings or the lookouts in the after gun tubs. I well knew that circumstance.

Most of the Dutch ship's crew and a few of the passengers were killed instantly but six or seven survived, getting into a lifeboat. In the swiftly lowering darkness, they saw an eleven-year-old boy jump into the water and swim to a life raft that had been automatically launched by the impact of the torpedo. He clambered up on top of it and was seen to be safe for a few minutes until the sub moved into the immediate scene, blocking the vision of those in the lifeboat including his mother.

After the sub skipper interrogated the occupants, the U-boat moved off into the night. The boy, who became Phillip of *The Cay,* my friend from Statesville childhood, couldn't be seen for the rest of the night. The people in the lifeboat rowed in ever-widening circles; shot up flares, shouted, did everything to attract his attention. But at first light in the morning, the face of the sea was empty. He was gone.

They kept rowing, hoping to at least find the life raft, but to no avail. They were rescued two days later by a tanker bound for Aruba. When the mother related the sad tale to the captain, he broke radio silence to call the Navy in Guantanamo Bay. Search planes were sent out but not even an oil slick where the ship had gone down could be found.

I had sailed the Caribbean enough to know what that child had faced besides fear: the constant pitching and tossing of the raft, the sun during the day, the cold water slopping aboard during the black night, sharks. Did he know there were stores in a big tin box under the trap door? Flares! Had the box jammed and he couldn't open it? Did he slide off the slick boards and become shark bait?

I quit *Fire on the Beaches* research that late morning to return to California, but the boy on the raft stayed with me for the next eleven years. I lived at the beach and walked it constantly with a dog. Sometimes I'd get a vision of the boy floating out there alone, praying to God for rescue. I didn't write *The Cay* until 1968 because I just wasn't ready to.

I reported to Perlberg and Seaton what I'd learned about the intelligence yarn. I wrote it up, including the fact that the Navy would be glad to cooperate as it did with their other Korean war story, Michener's *The Bridges at Toko-ri*.

The Tin Star, a western, was soon to start. I studied the script hoping to learn how to write one. Shooting outdoors on a movie ranch up in the San Fernando Valley, surrounded by horses and wranglers and stunt men, was my introduction to rolling cameras. What better place? The star Henry Fonda, a polite, retiring man, the ultimate professional, read a book between takes. In western costume, he remained in character off and on the set, moving in long, sometimes lazy strides, ever commanding in his role of sheriff. He seldom joked or smiled. Lessons one, two and three: Win the respect of towering artists like Henry Fonda. Let the relationship develop slow and easy. No surprises. No silly requests. No lies. Ahead were a few more like Fonda.

∾o∾

Try as he might, Perlberg could not develop the story of the Navy lieutenant in Korea. He signed several writers but it didn't jell. I took a shot at it, in spare time, and learned quickly that good screenwriting takes a different technique, an ability to think visually and beyond. I failed. Much later, I turned the story into a book for young readers, *The Children's War*, 1971, a work that I don't at all like. My characters were flawed.

Fire on the Beaches, the merchant marine U-boat saga, was published by W. W. Norton in the spring of 1958 to good reviews, affirming my own belief that I was capable of writing more than one book. No matter that you've been published twice or fifty times before, there is always a doubt: Can I do it again? You sweat and pray.

Next up were Clark Gable and Doris Day in *Teacher's Pet,* a newspaper story, Gable playing a tough metropolitan city editor and Day a journalism teacher. I wasn't at all sure how to approach Gable, he of Rhett Butler fame in *Gone With the Wind* and, though in his early fifties, still the Hollywood heartbeat and hunk. He was ranked among the top ten money-making stars from 1932 to 1955. He'd won an Academy Award for best actor. He'd been an Air Corps major in World War II. He'd earned everybody's respect. He was the most famous actor in the world. Young readers are advised to take a look at Mr. Gable via video.

As a kid, I'd seen him in *Hell Divers, China Seas, Mutiny on the Bounty, Call of the Wild,* and other rousing action-adventure films. As an adult, I'd seen him in *Across the Wide Missouri, Soldier of Fortune, Band of Angels.* He'd co-starred with the most beautiful and talented leading ladies in making more than fifty pictures. He was indeed Hollywood legend.

I had butterflies in my stomach when I first met him in Perlberg's office. The butterflies didn't arise down the line when I worked with Frank Sinatra, another but very different legend. Only with Gable did the little critters swarm around my gut. Later, I worked briefly in Barcelona with John Wayne, another legend. Over the years, I've borrowed bits and pieces of their very masculine characters for books. Drover, of *Walking Up a Rainbow,* 1986, has some John Wayne in him.

Having advanced from being a press agent, I was now included in all phases of Perlsea productions, from story buys to scriptwriter conferences, casting, music scoring, costumes, and other lessons, over time, that weren't listed in any "assistant's learning manual." It was an opportunity like none I'd ever had but I really didn't take advantage of it. Like my father, I had my own agenda. Quite simply, I wanted to be a book writer, not a movie worker.

My mother died of Parkinson's disease during the making of the next Gable film, and I flew home to Melbourne to accompany my father and her body to North Carolina. My brother-in-law, sister Louise's husband, had bought a family burial plot in Marion. No train berths were available on such short notice and we sat up all night, awaiting an opening, talking very little.

My father seemed to realize, finally, what he'd lost, as I did. He admitted, at one point, "She did not have a good life." That was the understatement of his own selfish life.

We had to change trains at about four o'clock in the morning and the big wooden box containing my mother's coffin was rolled out onto the chill platform for transfer to the regional line. Father and son stood on the platform near it, not saying a word, I remember. It was a scene from an old black-and-white movie. My sorrow was for her and not for him on the lonely road he'd now travel. The train's sad whistle at a crossing nearby as it drew away provided the background music.

At the church, I remember putting my mind on my own favorite scene: My mother preparing to bake an apple pie, her hands dipped in flour from rolling the crust, shouting, "Excelsior, excelsior!" onward and upward.

∽o∾

I felt that I had to attempt to help him get his life back together, so I invited him to stay with us for a while in Hollywood. Though Gwen didn't really know him that well, did not know his past, she agreed. His stay did not last long. He was interrupting the family and I had to ask him to leave, not a pleasant task.

He returned to Florida, sold his house and began to drift around the Southwest, only staying in one place long enough to receive his pension check. Through Louise I'd hear about him from time to time, imagining him in a run-down hotel lobby talking to other old men. He was now in his mid-seventies, yet I believed he was quite capable of taking care of himself. Any young tough who tried to grab his wallet would regret it. Any old man who got belligerent would end up on the floor. He walked a lot and exercised, she said. For peace of mind, I tried not to think of him but that was impossible. He was drifting around like the ghost ship *Mary Celeste* and I knew we'd meet again. Next up was *The Rat Race* with Tony Curtis and Debbie Reynolds.

∽o∾

Perlberg and Seaton had done several other pictures on location in Europe for several reasons—authenticity of background, authenticity of foreign bit players, and simply their own pleasure at working away from the nosy studio executives and enjoying the food and wines of the locales.

Now they were mounting *The Counterfeit Traitor,* featuring their favorite actor, Bill Holden, on locations in Germany, Denmark, and Sweden. Time over there was scheduled for at least six months. This World War II true story was based on the experiences of a Swedish businessman with access to Nazi Germany who became an Allied spy. The film would begin in West Berlin and then move to a studio in Hamburg for the summer, using sites in that heavily bombed city for outdoor locations; then to Copenhagen and Stockholm.

I hadn't been to Europe since the war and the prospect of working in Germany, Copenhagen, and Stockholm, living over there on company expense was beyond alluring. I'd been told I could buy a car, on the company, then keep it. This way they wouldn't have to provide a car and driver, which would cost them even more money. I could bring my family over after making a deal with Lufthansa German Airlines for a documentary. *Ah, the picture business.*

More than ten years after the war there were parts of both East and West Berlin that were still in rubble, one reason we were shooting there. The Reichstag looked much like it had in the last days of Hitler; Templehof Airport, almost in the middle of the city, looked much the same; the Brandenburg Gate, passage to East Berlin, was pock-marked but substantially the same. I couldn't wait. The locations would provide background for *books. My books!*

The first day's shooting was along the banks of the Spree River in West Berlin. The Communists, likely tipped-off by a phone call, sent their patrol boats out to interrupt the filming. It became a game in which we hid cameras, made phony set-ups, and otherwise tried to cope with an enemy. It took three days to do one day's work. Welcome to the Cold War.

After twelve days of mainly exteriors, I rolled for Hamburg along the autobahn that went through East German territory. The top echelon flew to avoid any possibility of being detained by the Communists. My new green VW convertible purred from guard stop to guard stop at such places as Wollin, Ziesar, Barleban, and Marienborn, breaking into West Germany at Helmstadt. I made due note of that trip and its stops, for possible later fiction treatment. I remember the guards, with their cold eyes, mostly blue, and their expressionless faces, enviously inspecting the spanking new car and its monied American owner. I was relieved to cross the border. Adding to my personal income I made the film-connected documentary for Lufthansa, producing, writing, and directing it while tending to my other chores.

My family arrived to spend the summer in Europe and I could introduce them to foreign film locales. They visited the sets and Mark became an "extra." I did not realize I was internationalizing the children forever, turning them into avid travelers ready to catch the next jet to somewhere. It paid off handsomely and I decided to do it on all future foreign locales.

Dating back to the silent movie days, directors and producers have used historic and familiar landmarks as backgrounds. From the shattered Reichstag in Berlin to the Grand Hotel in Stockholm, Seaton's camera roamed visually. Those of us lucky enough to work on the black-and-white film, a rarity at this time of color cinema, sampled the flavors, smells, sights, and sounds. I appropriated them for the later adult novel, *The Stalker,* 1987.

ᦲᦵᦲ

Back at Paramount, now 1961, I read a book by a British author, *Night Without End,* and convinced Messrs. P & S that it would make a good suspense picture. I further convinced Perlberg to permit me a shot at doing the screenplay. I'd been their student for six years and certainly had picked up some knowledge. He agreed.

For the next five months, over and above my regular "assisting" work, I labored over the screenplay, doing three or four drafts, and finally had my secretary type a final draft. I submitted it to Perlberg and, without reading it, he said, "Put Bill, Jr.'s name on it, too." His adopted son had finished college and had joined the staff as assistant to me. He was a fine young man but hadn't written a word of the screenplay. That kind of Hollywood family theft had been going on for years. Pure nepotism.

I was shocked. I was speechless. Leaving his office I went back to my own and sat for about two hours. Then I went by Seaton's office, told him what had happened and told him I was resigning. I thanked him for all he'd done, then went back to Perlberg's office, thanked him, too, and quit. Shades of my father but I didn't punch the boss.

Living within walking distance of the studio, near Hancock Park, I went home slowly, thinking about what I'd tell Gwen. The money milk cow had just left the pasture. Vanished! Gone! All within the past few hours. As a mother and wife, she did not take the news kindly. Another son, Michael, had been born not too long before. What I considered principle, Gwen considered foolish. I said bravely, "I'll freelance." I remember her laughing caustically.

It was difficult to blame Gwen. Was I going to sell to *Grit, Male, Men,* and *Stag* and support a family? I now had faith in myself, in my ability, but it would take quite a long while before I could bring my income back to the Paramount level, seven-fifty a week.

And there was another part: We'd gone to some lavish film-connected parties, studio and Academy screenings, rubbed elbows with Gable, Holden and the like, were photographed with them. She loved that life. All over! Looking far back, I think our marriage began to unravel that late afternoon below Hollywood and Vine. Even before, looking back, we'd had some classic quarrels. I accept equal blame. I was an obsessed writer, possessed with my typewriter.

I took my typewriter out to a garden shack behind the garage and began work on a novella entitled *A Test of Faith*, an adult story about a phony miracle involving blood being accidentally dripped on a wooden statue of Christ. It quickly sold to *Redbook Magazine* for six thousand dollars as their back-of-the-book offering. The story was optioned three times over the years by different Hollywood producers, but studios declined to put up any money in the end. Ten years later I decided to expand it to a full novel, entitling it *The Maldonado Miracle.* The miraculous ending of that story will be told later.

We sold the Hollywood house and moved to Laguna Beach, an artists' colony. Romantically, a small town by the Pacific Ocean sands south of Los Angeles was where a writer should be. Well, wasn't it? I set up my typewriter in a cubicle on the ground floor of an old Mother Goose house with a 120 degree sea view.

Three anxious months had passed and I was pounding the typewriter daily when my wife flatly declared, "You have to get a job!" The six thousand from *Redbook* was running out.

Oh, ye of little faith, I thought. *Ye of no faith.* Probably legions of freelance writers have faced this jerked-out rug. When the freelancer is also the family provider, self-faith and worth are shaken and fear becomes naked, particularly when there are no calls from New York announcing a sale. I'd started to work on another book, *Threepersons,* based on a true person. No advance. It was a western, set on the El Paso border.

The quickest way to money was to reluctantly put on my flack suit again, a bitter fitting. Humbly, I called a friend at Columbia Pictures and offered my services at $350 weekly, four hundred less than Paramount. A picture entitled *Diamond Head,* starring Charlton Heston, would be getting underway soon in Kauai. If I had to earn ready cash, why not Hawaii?

On the long flight to Honolulu I bounced the future around in my head and came to what seemed a sensible solution. Be a part-time freelancer for a while: work a picture, either in publicity or production or make a documentary, take the good Hollywood money and let it finance the writing of a book for the other part of the year. Selfishly, of course, I wanted to spend the entire year in my writer's sanctuary, safe from the real world—the world of wives and children.

Diamond Head was somewhat an uncooked turkey—the producer couldn't have carried Perlberg's briefcase and the British director couldn't have held Seaton's watch. But Chuck Heston was easygoing and the leading lady was having an affair with the director, her mind totally consumed with love, so it all went well.

Midway through location filming, I received a call from Lufthansa. They wanted another Hollywood-themed travelogue to be filmed in Madrid, Paris, Athens, Rome, Munich, and London. They'd meet all production costs, plus pay a healthy fee, ten thousand. I'd write and direct. I figured five shooting weeks plus three weeks editing and adding narration and music. Eight more weeks away from the typewriter, but in the new scheme of things, the money would provide writing time for three or four months. Get it while I could! Rejoice! Smile! Even laugh!

Finishing up *Diamond Head* at Columbia, I went home to begin pecking away on *Threepersons*. The writing pattern was set that year of 1962. I didn't know how long it would take, how many books I would have to write, until I could say a final good-bye to the flicks, but at least I had time frames to work with and food and all the other necessities to sustain the family.

Early in the life of a desperately money-grubbing freelancer, it pays to learn that the work at hand is not at all sacred. My wife's get-a-job clock would soon start to tick again, so I decided to try and compress *Threepersons* into a TV hour.

Only about forty pages of that book had come out of the type-writer, but I knew the beginning, the middle, and the end of the story, truthful elements that I'd thoroughly researched: In 1921, a former Indian gunfighter named Tom Threepersons became deputy sheriff of El Paso and went to war against bootleggers running their wares across the Rio Grande nightly. At the time, bossed by a crooked politician, El Paso was worse than the Chicago gangland. Threepersons had to revert back to his gunfighting days to win the war.

I sold the script to Universal for a Kraft Mystery Theater hour and rode the freeway to Studio City for a conference with the director. I was barely seated when he said, "Make the Indian the heavy!"

Was he crazy? Was he on pot? I angrily said, "Are you smoking it?" which he didn't appreciate. I can't even remember his name. *Threepersons* aired on NBC pretty much as written and the budding novel wasn't damaged in any way. I was six thousand richer.

∽∾∽

I did the Lufthansa travelogue with a Danish cameraman and an Academy Award-caliber film editor who came along for the lark, not the small salary. Her contribution in suggesting camera angles was monumental. Then back to the El Paso novel.

Again needing money, I ducked out for two months to do *Major Dundee,* starring Charlton Heston and the late British actor Richard Harris, to be filmed almost entirely in Mexico, with locations in Durango, Cuernavaca, Chilpancingo, and Mexico City. I contracted with Columbia to write and direct a behind-the-scenes promotional short on stuntmen. Extra money. I flew the family down. They enjoyed Heston and Harris.

Dundee's director was the late, highly talented, Sam Peckinpah, maker of such classic westerns as *The Wild Bunch* and *Ride the High Country.* Sam loved violence for the sake of violence and bred it. The benign Heston once threatened him with a cavalry sabre. I saw a fist-fight between Sam and the producer.

I remember one morning on the sweltering greenish Chilpancingo River when he staged ride-bys, twenty or thirty Mexican extras on Indian ponies. He sat on the camera platform, laughing, tossing movie blood in their faces. He was doing it for jollies. The camera wasn't even rolling. Along with some other reasonable observers I thought he was insane.

Durango was still the old "shoot 'em up" west. I witnessed a real revenge killing during night filming at a fort that Columbia had built several miles outside the city. Another time, on a Sunday morning when I was having breakfast with my secretary at the Hotel Duran, a drunken Mexican army major shot a tray-carrying waiter to death not twenty feet from us for no good reason. A typical

Peckinpah scene, though real. Adriana said, "We should go." I swiftly agreed.

The movie business was adding to my idea portfolio continually; adding to my knowledge of foreign locales that might or might not be used for one book or another. Admittedly, I was using the job for my own purposes but I tried very hard to deliver more than was required on any film. Apparently I was successful because I had no problem finding work at any studio in town. I continued my selfish ways of overseas work, getting away from domestic battles.

After *Dundee's* wild convolutions there were behind-the-scenes shorts for United Artists and Paramount with subjects ranging from Bob Hope and favorite artist Norman Rockwell to a pretty German circus aerialist. Hiring a cameraman, I did the writing and directing and editing.

In what other profession than the mixture of writing and the movies could you meet and work with a famous comedian and an artist whose paintings will live on for generations, all within a period of six weeks? The money was lovely.

My father died at eighty-seven in the veteran's hospital in Asheville, North Carolina, where the family had once lived. He had a hernia operation in the morning and was walking the halls in the afternoon, strong as King Kong. He passed away three days later from complications. Just before his death he bragged that it took six orderlies to hold him down. That was my father.

In the fall of 1964, I flew from Taipei, Taiwan, to Tokyo's Narita Airport to make sure that Steve McQueen would show up on schedule for his scenes in *The Sand Pebbles,* a Robert Wise production for Twentieth Century-Fox. McQueen had a well-deserved reputation for being difficult, and Wise, an Oscar winner for *West Side Story* and a shoo-in for *The Sound of Music* at the next Academy Award ceremonies, was concerned. Millions were going to be spent on *Sand Pebbles* and he thought McQueen needed kid-glove handling. I was jack-of-all-trades on that film, and wanted an Oriental background for a book. I had no idea what it would be.

I'd met the bad-boy star briefly in the Beverly Hills studio but I was certain he didn't remember my face or name. That made little difference. What would make a difference was his overnight suite at the swank Okura Hotel, the limo from Narita to Tokyo, and paying attention to his every wish. I hired an interpreter just in case there were unforeseen problems. His wife, former Broadway star Neilie Adams, and their two small children were accompanying him.

The JAL jet landed on time and I stood by the customs and immigration interior wire fence, watching from there as the McQueens began the usual procedure of entering a foreign country. No more than three minutes passed until all hell broke loose during the customs inspection. There was shouting between McQueen and the small group around the baggage table. I said to the interpreter, "Go find out what's wrong."

He scurried back in a moment. "Mr. McQueen has a gun."

Oh, dear Lord! Bringing a weapon into Japan was like bringing in the plague. I said, "Find some way to get there and tell McQueen I'm out here. Tell the customs people not to have him arrested. Tell them they can hold the gun overnight and give it to China Airlines in the morning. Go!"

It took almost an hour, with the interpreter shuttling back and forth between me at the steel wire fence and the customs people, but finally they agreed to let the family go and to keep the weapon in customs and turn it over to the pilot in the morning.

Finally, he came over to the fence and said, "Who are you?"

I gave him my name and told him I was representing Bob Wise and Fox.

He said, "I want six guards in the hotel corridor."

"No problem," I said to his retreating back, thinking I'd love to belt him.

I told the interpreter to call the Okura and get six of the biggest armed Japanese bodyguards they could find at this time of night and have them on display when we reached the hotel. I'd pay double. In Hollywood, with a contretemps like this one, money is never considered. If the leading man or lady is angry, sulky, or unreasonable with their first scene just two days ahead, *spend the money* and smile.

In the limo, hardly speaking to me, he said, "You know why I brought the gun?"

I said, "No."

He said, "So my children won't be kidnapped."

His children were in a thousand times more danger in the San Fernando Valley than in Japan. I said, "I understand."

McQueen had spent some of his youth in reform schools, had large explosive chips on his shoulder, all of which had nothing to do with his ability as an actor. His talents were exceptional.

The movie was about a U.S. naval gunboat, the *San Pablo*, on the Yangtze and co-starred Richard Crenna, Richard Attenborough, and Candace Bergen (well known as TV's *Murphy Brown*). The schedule was long and difficult, both in Taiwan and Hong Kong.

Robert Wise has the patience of the Dalai Lama and got along well with McQueen while cameras were rolling, but off-stage the bull-headed actor kept Fox and Wise in turmoil. He bought a big Kawasaki motorcycle and rode it around Taipei as if he was in a circus act. The insurance company threatened to pull its entire production policy. There was always something off-stage that drove the production staff and myself to indigestion. Neilie McQueen tried to control him but usually didn't succeed. I once rode the Kawasaki sitting behind him at 90 mph down Taiwan roads he'd never seen. Heart in mouth.

Over the next months, I'd get an occasional midnight or later call from Steve's wife, "He's on the loose!" I'd draw a thousand USA dollars from the hotel and go out to find him, knowing several of his likely bars. Once, I missed him by only a few minutes but found the Chinese man he'd decked. I asked the bartender what had happened. He said, "This fellow asked Steve for his autograph." The "fellow" was nursing a split lip and I apologized for McQueen and shelled out five hundred dollars to avoid a possible assault arrest.

My main job, in addition to troubleshooting, was to shoot behind-the-scenes shorts for both theatrical, mainly in Europe, and TV release. I always wrote an outline and then broadened it while filming. In this case, the main subject was the gunboat, a reasonable duplicate of the old USS *San Pablo,* built in Hong Kong. With film, I followed it across the South China Sea to the Straits of Formosa and then to the Tamsui River, subbing for the wide Yangtze. China, of course, would not allow any American film company anywhere near the mainland. Two big wooden junks were also built for the camera's eyes. Smaller craft were also used. The Yangtze of the 1920s came to life.

In contrast to the insanity and anarchy of *Major Dundee, The Sand Pebbles* was picture-making at its best, Wise always in firm control of both cast and crew on the set. I loved working with him and with suave and polished Richard Attenborough and equally polished Richard Crenna. It took a while with McQueen. Candy Bergen seemed a little lost in this, her second film. Her role as a young missionary did not require the hidden talent she revealed in *Murphy Brown*.

Most of all I loved prowling Taipei at night in an old Buick with my constant companion, a former driver at the U.S. Embassy. I'd hired Jimmy Chang because of his knowledge of the city and his ability to speak English. I was already thinking about that novel set in Taipei and he seemed amused at all my research questions, as well as my insistence on trying the foods of all the mainland provinces now represented in Taiwan. We ate well.

I flew my family to the *Sand Pebbles* location in early December, renting an apartment next to a rice paddy where water buffalo roamed. The children were introduced to Taiwan with a thirty-foot string of firecrackers provided by my beaming driver. From that morning on they were immersed in all things Chinese.

Mark often accompanied me to the filming sets, particularly when I had my own "second unit" crew at work.

One early morning, on Chungking North Road, traffic swarming, Jimmy halted at a stoplight and I looked over to see my eleven-year-old daughter sitting nonchalantly in a pedicab, a three-wheeled bicycle taxi. I was certain her mother didn't know she was out alone. I yelled at Wendy and she waved back. I said, "Jimmy, pull over. That's my daughter, Wendy." He smiled at me, the one gold tooth glittering, "She'll be fine," he said, waving to the pedaler, and put the car in gear. That spirit of adventure has continued her entire life.

When not riding in the Buick I often roamed on foot Chungking North Road and other streets in the noisy, smoky city, just as I'd prowled Statesville as a kid. Hundreds of pedicabs jangled around and what seemed to be ten thousand motorbikes, puffing choking exhaust, wheeled in and out of traffic. I watched the sidewalk dentists, with their tubs of extracted teeth, at work. I listened to the haunting whistles of the blind masseurs as they tapped their way along the streets at night; I even used one as a killer in *The Body Trade,* 1964, set in Taiwan and Mainland China. I tried to capture the sights and sounds and smells of the Orient.

After five months on the Tamsui, the *San Pablo* was towed to the New Territories, in Hong Kong, for battle scenes. To move an entire motion picture company—cast, crew; props, costumes, cameras, lights—is similar to moving an army. About two weeks was required to make the shift before "Light 'em up" was heard.

I completed filming the international TV documentary, *A Ship Called San Pablo,* to be narrated by Attenborough, with the battle scenes between the gunboat sailors and Chinese soldiers. I'd supervise editing, narration and music at the Fox studio.

∽∘∾

Out of all this movie madness I was beginning to see a faint rosy glow on the horizon. Over the past ten years I'd sold the Mitscher book, then *Fire on the Beaches,* ghosted four books, written two novellas, and sold about a dozen short stories to national magazines and an equal number of nonfiction travel pieces. *The Saturday Evening Post, Redbook, McCall's, Argosy*, and other periodicals of the time had issued checks. But more than the money, there was an indication by sales alone that I was finally learning how to write. It had taken me an awfully long time since the first bylined *Portsmouth Star* story in 1934. I was now middle-aged but grayness of scalp was not catching up as yet.

Usually, I sit on an idea for a few or many years before attacking it, letting the seeds stay in my unconscious, hoping they'll suddenly burst forth as good fruit. Arriving back in Laguna from the Far East, full of fresh memories, I wrote *The Body Trade*. A rich Newport couple with a ding-a-ling daughter who'd defected to the Chinese Red Guard hires John Amber, a disgraced ex-CIA agent, to fetch her home. He uses exotic Taipei as his base of operations. I'd worked on the novel mentally during the *Sand Pebbles* location and blew the dust off my typewriter almost immediately.

∞○∞

I wrote seven days a week for almost three months before shipping it to the agency, having inherited highly regarded Armitage Watkins, of New York, from the Mitscher book. I probably have set some kind of record by being with the same agency, now owned by Gloria Loomis, for fifty years. I may be one of the most loyal writers on earth.

The Body Trade sold to Fawcett, and I gained the satisfaction of knowing that I could indeed write a novel. It was an ordinary suspense story and got a few lines in the *New York Times Book Review,* not too complimentary but citing the surprise ending. Good enough. It was briefly considered by Fox. I've had at least fifteen properties optioned by film companies. Only four have been produced.

For the balance of 1966 and 1967, I stayed home, where a father and husband should be. Mark once asked, "Why are you away so often?" I lied, saying, "We need the income." In truth, I was avoiding the frequent spats and silences.

When I was home, then and other times, I tried to involve the children with what I was doing, taking them on school visits and bookstore signings; talking about writing. But it did not compensate for the weeks and sometimes months that I was away. I knew that.

I made several more documentary films, then wrote a non-fiction book entitled *People Who Make Movies,* which was adopted by the University of Southern California cinema arts school as a text. Avon bought it for a paperback edition.

Easy to write, each chapter was devoted to one of the jobs required to make a film: actors, producer, director, composer, down to the set decorators, grips, electricians, stuntmen. I had access to experts at any given studio and interviewed them. Reviews were surprisingly good. *Saturday Review* said, "There isn't an acid personal remark in the book...," as if Hollywood couldn't be interpreted without venom. Two nonfiction sea collections followed the movie book.

In 1967 Wendy acquired a male yellow Labrador pup which she named Brandy Golden Boy. Big of paw, with a chest that eventually reached fifteen inches wide, Brandy was a lover and could somehow sense a bitch in heat within a radius of several blocks. I have no idea how many puppies he fathered, but there would be phone calls from a people a mile away, "Would you please come and get your dog." Once, on the beach, I had to separate him from a Collie lady without benefit of a water hose. The owner was jumping up and down in outrage.

Brandy quickly became my writing pal and would come down the inside stairs of our beachfront house and flop himself at my feet until it was time to walk. Our love affair developed quickly and naturally. He became the sightless model for *The Trouble with Tuck,* 1986. I am a hopeless lover of dogs.

∽o∾

I estimated, without any real reason, I was three films away from escaping the motion picture business, my port of refuge in financial and marital squalls. Fox called to offer me a pair of Frank Sinatra films, back to back. *The Detective* would be filmed in New York, and *The Lady in Cement* would be filmed in Miami Beach. "Sinatra?" After a pause, I said, "I've really got to think about it." Away from home again, *danger!*

Taking on Sinatra and all the violent intrigues that often surrounded him, even if I got along with Ol' Blue Eyes, did not seem very smart. Why hadn't they offered a Gregory Peck or Bill Holden picture in Hollywood? Yet the back-to-back aspect appealed to me. I'd previously turned down Columbia's offer to do a Brando and a Streisand. Ulcers I did not want.

There was that other reason, beyond immediate income for going to New York and Florida, the same reason that had sent me to Taiwan and the other places above. It would be an escape from the fierce home battling which never seemed to end. I was, in fact, repeating what my often absentee father had done, though strife at home had never sent him away. There had been no strife other than that which he created.

Admittedly, during the last brace of years, I'd thought of divorce now and then but filing those papers was something I knew I'd never do, simply because of the children. Gwen had first mentioned legal recourse in our third year of marriage after she'd spent a month visiting her mother in San Francisco. She told me the night she flew in, "I've thought about divorcing you. I'm not having any fun here." Neither was I.

Deeply in love as a new husband, I'd missed her very much and was shocked at her casual mention of the hateful word. Unfortunately, that night, that scene high over the Hudson River, lingered in my head over the years, festering, breeding insecurity, never completely erased. It undermined the years ahead.

There'd never been a divorce in my mother's family, I knew, and none of my sisters had undergone the ordeal. Naoma's marriage had been annulled after her preacher husband was declared insane. Pride was involved but I thought more about our children than any other aspect. I was wrong because they were in the front row of conflict. I was wrong not to face the inevitable for so many years. I was cowardly.

Gwen had grown up without a father, her mother having divorced several times. She did not seem to have a fear of the deed.

The Detective was going to be made entirely on location in New York and *The Lady in Cement* would have the same treatment in Miami Beach. "Frank will also be singing at the Fontainebleau down there at night," the studio said. I'd have nothing to do with those octaves.

The Detective was going to be the first hard look at a cop's life in the big city, a very gritty look. It was the story of a burnt-out NYPD detective who sends the wrong man to the electric chair for murdering a homosexual. He loses both his job and his nympho wife, played by Lee Remick. Though he had a second-rate director, one he could dictate to, Sinatra did a good job. It was his kind of film.

What was happening off-stage was also pure Sinatra. After Ava Gardner, he'd married twenty-one-year-old Mia Farrow at age fifty-three. It was just one year later, and the marriage was already at end. She was making *Rosemary's Baby* at Paramount and he'd demanded that she quit and join his own cast in New York. Mia said no, a word that Sinatra never wanted to hear. He filed for divorce without telling her.

It was a media bombshell that blew on the eve of "Scene 1, Take 1" and there was a near riot on West 79th Street when his limo pulled up to the shouts of "Frank, Frank, is it true?" Three big goons ran interference for him through reporters, photographers, and news cameramen. I was knocked around like a tackling dummy. TV trucks were there.

Sinatra had not sought publicity, *of any kind,* for years, and the

New York press was in a feeding frenzy. Poor, lovely Lee Remick might have just as well been making *Wind in the Willows.* I got phone calls at my hotel at night from gossip columnists, "You hear Frank say anything about Mia today?" Not a word, I'd answer, truthfully. To my utter delight, my only job was to be there in case someone had a question that didn't deal with Frank Sinatra.

Robert Duval, one of the finest actors in the world, made one of his first screen appearances in the precinct scenes, displaying the raw talent that has since been polished into a number of extraordinary performances, including the Academy nominee *Apostle*, 1997. I spent time talking to him and co-star Jack Klugman. Otherwise I silently observed Mr. Sinatra day after day. He was a case study like none other. I didn't see him at night, unless there were night street scenes. Characters of suspect occupation often visited the sets, and after shooting was over, he'd vanish.

The Mia Farrow tempest had not died away by the time filming was completed, and I gladly went home for the holidays to be with my family and to look at the Christmas tree instead of swarthy goons. I was tempted to call Fox and get them to assign someone else to *The Lady in Cement,* which was certain to be a barnyard species. Sinatra would star as detective Tony Rome.

The opening shot of the film was of a blonde nude, her feet encased in a block of cement on the bottom of Biscayne Bay. Judging from the script, the story went down, not up, from there. Raquel Welch, making her second film, was co-starring.

I arrived at the Hotel Fontainebleau the day before Sinatra flew in and met him in the lobby, asking if I could be of help. *Cement* wouldn't start for three or four days. "Yeah, take my calls." I knew that was temporary. One of his own staff would tend to that when they showed up. His "calls" were interesting, to say the least.

We conversed only when he wanted something. Fine with me.

Filming of *The Lady in Cement* began at the Fontainebleau and the first day was a disaster. Raquel Welch was frightened of Sinatra and well she should be. She kept blowing her lines and Sinatra, always preferring one take then moving on to the next scene, became angrier by the minute. It wasn't a good start. Sinatra disappeared. Photography of the scene was stopped and pick-up shots were made.

Along with five or six other members of the crew, I went back to my hotel. All of us were headed for the bar, which was directly across the lobby from the main door. I never got there.

In the middle of the lobby were about a dozen black people singing spirituals around a grand piano. I stopped to listen. I knew that the Southern Christian Leadership Conference was having a regional meeting at the hotel. I hadn't heard spirituals like these since my mother took me to the black church in Statesville. For a moment I thought Dr. Martin Luther King was one of the singers, but then realized it was someone who looked quite a lot like him.

I stayed there until they finished singing and then went up to my room and ordered dinner. After the sleaze of both the detective pictures, I thought it was now time to do something else, time to write the story of that Dutch boy who floated away from the torpedoed ship in 1942 and was never seen again. It was time to give him a life.

TIME TO WRITE

The Cay wrote itself. I began the first words not long after returning from Miami in mid-March, 1968. It had been more than a decade since I'd come across the translated account of the Dutch ship being torpedoed in the Caribbean. All I did was feed paper into the machine. The book had already formed in my subconscious.

I remember that my first problem was to find someone capable of rescuing the eleven-year-old boy off his raft. I'd sailed with three West Indians on the *Castana* and I'd met an elderly St. Thomian named Robbert, his only name. I'd listened to his stories about childhood in the Virgin Islands and his experiences in the Caribbean on schooners. I'd shared rum with him, fished with him. The character of Timothy in the novel was based on Robbert, with smaller parts of the other two *Castana* sailors mixed in. Robbert knew more about the Caribbean than any man I'd ever been around.

I refuse to write about people I don't know about. But I didn't know any Dutch boys then and I don't know any now, so I went back to my own childhood to find an American boy to replace the one who was lost. I remembered the Statesville kid I'd played with when I was five or six until I was ten. With his mother-taught hating of anyone with black skin, it occurred to me that it might be interesting if I put Phillip on that raft with a black man upon whom his very life would depend. Then purposely blinded the boy so that by book's end he might be truly colorblind. I did not think at length about it. Rather, that condition was a thought out of nowhere that occurred at the typewriter. I never outline fiction, fearing I'll follow the outline. My only course is to use real people as models. Why invent?

The book was written, without effort, in three weeks, and I dedicated it to Martin Luther King. Sold immediately to Doubleday, several weeks later John Ernst, the senior editor of books for young readers, called to tell me that he thought it was a "fine work." I was then pecking away on another book and he caught me in mid-paragraph. I barely acknowledged his nice words. I'd never written a book for young readers.

Very little editing was done, although at one point I wanted to change the beginning, open with the torpedoing of the ship. Ernst said he thought it should be left the way it was, a quiet beginning. He was right.

I really did not know what I'd written. I thought of it as a simple adventure story with a subtle message about the tragedy of racial prejudice, hence the King dedication. I honestly paid no attention to it. No one was more surprised at what was about to happen to *The Cay* than I was.

I went back to work on the Texas border novel, *Threepersons,* off-and-on writing that had been defying me for years. I could not nail down the Indian's character.

∽o∾

At forty-five minutes past midnight, June 5, 1968, in the Rampart Division of the Los Angeles Police Department, Sgt. William C. Jordan sat facing a slight, dark-haired young man who had just been brought into the station as the suspect in the shooting of Senator Robert F. Kennedy.

The news of the tragic event was already being broadcast around the world. Stunned and disbelieving, men and women heard that life was ebbing away in the young man whose brother, the president, had been assassinated. After hearing of the killing of Dr. Martin Luther King, Senator Kennedy had quoted Aeschylus: "In our sleep, pain which cannot forget falls drop by drop upon our heart, until in our own despair, against our will, comes wisdom through the awful grace of God." Now the Senator himself had been struck down.

Having seen a TV clip of the shooting that night, unable to believe it had really happened, I remember driving toward Los Angeles on the freeway to edit a documentary in the morning, seeing headlights burning everywhere in a tribute to Senator Kennedy, I turned on mine.

I can't remember when I received the call from agent Armitage Watkins asking if I was interested in teaming with Robert Houghton, chief of detectives of LAPD, for the purpose of a book on the Kennedy killing. The only meager police reporting I'd ever done had been with the Virginia and West Virginia papers. I was told that the Random House editor had read *The Magnificent Mitscher;* I was also within easy driving distance of the LAPD and I knew Houghton from a single fishing trip out of Newport. Yes, I was very much interested. Expanding horizons is a good thing to do. So began an adventure like none I'd ever had.

Big, genteel Robert Houghton, a career cop with degrees in psychology and sociology, was determined that his investigation would not be shamefully fumbled the way Dallas had mishandled the President Kennedy assassination investigation. He told all of his detectives that he wanted every single interview and interrogation *recorded*; not one was to be written. He was listening to every word.

I talked to him for hours before eventually lugging home about 5,000 separate taped interrogations, 50,000 pages of other documentation and material evidence, 1,700 photographs, and 20 reels of 16 mm film. Already the conspiracy theorists were crawling out from under their usual rocks, intent on exploiting the Kennedy name.

My garage, up a stairway from the beach, was covered with aspects of the Robert Kennedy investigation, and I struggled with the sheer bulk of it. There were FBI and CIA documents—especially the latter, which I shouldn't have seen but Houghton decided that the book must be based on every possible source of evidence.

One evening he brought down additional papers from the ongoing investigation, and when he opened the trunk of his car I saw a riot gun and his bullet-proof vest. I'd become so familiar with his easy-going manner that I'd forgotten he was, first of all, a cop.

Finally, Houghton decided that there was no conspiracy, that Sirhan Bishara Sirhan, a Palestinian, had acted alone in Senator Kennedy's death: motive, Kennedy's known support of Israel. More than a dozen "conspiracy" books have been written since the publication of *Special Unit Senator*, but none have proved, much less named, one or more other killers. I'm quite proud of the Houghton-Taylor effort, which was widely praised. "From it emerges a sense of the magnitude and depth of problems encountered in police work." - *The Los Angeles Times*. There was not a single negative review. Sirhan was the first Islamic terrorist to act in the United States.

Copies of *The Cay* began going out to reviewers, contest judges, and other interested parties in early spring, 1969, with official publication set for June. Doubleday had high hopes for the book, I was told. I spoke before a group of nationwide sales reps.

The publisher flew me to Dallas to speak and sign autographs at the annual American Library Association convention. As a first-time juvenile author, I was amazed at all the effort over one little book. They were going to give away 750 hardbacks to generate "talk" about *The Cay* and make it a contender for the coveted Newbery Award.

I was sitting down on the convention floor, pen-in-hand, innocently signing away when an agitated woman, her face reddened and contorted, shouted something about racism and spat at me. She wasn't even in line. Her name plate said she was from New York City. Beyond shock, I was frozen in my seat. Someone standing nearby gave me a Kleenex and I wiped my cheek as she was hustled away. For a moment, I thought about leaving the floor in an effort to regain composure. The Doubleday salesman who was helping with the line said, "Are you all right?" Then he whispered, "She's crazy!"

In truth, I was tongue-tied. This had happened at ALA with fifteen or sixteen thousand book people present. Librarians, sellers, writers, illustrators. Not a likely place for ugliness. Was it something personal? I was not a racist! I didn't have time to even think about sorting it out. Most writers try to say a few words while signing, to smile and be pleasant. I didn't do very well for what time remained.

I had thought that *The Cay* was just a gentle adventure book without any axe, *of any kind*, to grind. During the writing I really had no idea that I was dealing with a subject considered explosive by some individuals and some organizations, especially the Interracial Council on Children's Books, a vitriolic, self-serving group based in New York.

The incident was talked about at length during dinner that night and one of the Doubleday salesmen said, "Sometimes the writer doesn't know what's in the book." I found that hard to believe but in this case it was true. The "racism" charge widened monthly. I was heartsick.

In the fall of 1969, I promised myself that *Tora! Tora! Tora!*, the Pearl Harbor air raid story, was going to be my last motion picture; that I was going to stay home, write, and attempt to resolve the intermittent warfare that was destroying my marriage. Enough money was beginning to come in from writing to support us modestly without the need of Hollywood paychecks. Fox signed me to be the producer's assistant at fifteen hundred dollars weekly.

The scope of the film was staggering. Recreating Japan's preparations to raid Pearl Harbor required building a section of the carrier *Akagi* on the island of Kyushu. A section of the USS *Arizona* would have to be built on two barges in Pearl Harbor. The attacking

Japanese aircraft would not be miniatures—actual aircraft converted to look like the real planes would be used. As the script was finished, none of us involved realized just how mammoth and far-flung *Tora! Tora! Tora!* (Tiger! Tiger! Tiger!—Attack! Attack! Attack!) would be. Or just how expensive. Or, sadly, how tragic. Two pilots were killed before the film started. I saw one of them crash and die.

The huge American unit to film the sequences of the raid—everything was huge—would be based in Honolulu. Interiors of the Washington involvement would be done at the studio. Unlike the 2001 movie *Pearl Harbor,* it was to be an authentic documentary, no love story. Famed Akira Kurosawa, Japan's legendary director of *Seven Samurai* and *Rashomon,* sometimes named the world's finest film-maker, would create his nation's sequences. The Japanese government had agreed to cooperate only if the exact truth was told.

Four Americans, including myself and my secretary, Doris Spriggs, (who held the same job on *The Sand Pebbles*) formed our unit. A bright Londoner, Doris had worked all over the world on both British and American films. She was the glue, and my savior. We were supposed to ride "herd" on Kurosawa-san, a laughable assignment. No one told Kurosawa-san what to do.

Our base of operations was Toei Studios in Kyoto, the city of shrines, practically the only city in Japan that had not been bombed during World War II. None of us could speak Japanese. We were at the mercy of interpreters. I thought to myself, "What are any of us doing here?" Gwen, Wendy, and Michael joined me for the holidays. Mark was a deckhand, fishing off Mexico.

Michael was then eight and deeply interested in electronics. Thinking that would be a wonderful career for him, I approved heartily. Coming home from the studio in mid-afternoon on Christmas Eve I discovered that none of the elevators at the Hotel Kyoto were running. In preparing our suite for the next morning, the tree already in place, Michael had blown the entire electrical system. Of course, this upset management, as well as other guests. I went around saying, "*Gomen-nasai; sumi-masen,*" an apologetic look on my face.

Kurosawa worked when he wanted to work, not by any Hollywood schedule, and that was reported back to the studio. Why didn't we just give Kurosawa the money and let him make his part of the film his way? That wasn't our American way. Pressure was applied to him and he became angry and started drinking heavily. One night he took his fist and broke out all windows in the sound stage. The great artist Kurosawa-san was just being himself. The gleeful Japanese press was reporting every minute of the battle between their film giant and the unworthies in Hollywood.

Every day at Toei I smiled and nodded but knew it would take a thousand years for any of us to understand this closed society.

We'd hired Minoru Genda, the naval officer who had planned the raid, and the lead pilot, Mitsuo Fuchida, as technical advisors. Genda was now a retired lieutenant general in the Japanese armed forces after helping General Douglas MacArthur with occupation problems. Fuchida was a Christian minister. Along with their government, both men had been responsible for killing 2,403 Americans, including civilians, and wounding another 1,178.

I lunched with them at a little restaurant a block away from the Toei studio. They spoke excellent English. One of the first questions I asked Genda was, "How do you feel about your role at Pearl Harbor?"

He answered, "I was a military man under military orders. My regret was that I didn't take out the submarine base and the oil storage tanks. Midway might not have happened." Midway was the turning-point battle for the United States. He was correct—without immediate fuel, the ships could not have sailed. I had to pinch myself mentally, realizing I was lunching with the man who planned the raid on Pearl Harbor.

Tora! Tora! Tora! costing $45,000,000, was one of the most expensive films ever made up to that time. There was no chance that it would ever return the dollars and yen spent on its production.

THE BATTLE OF *THE CAY*

Time to time, looking back, I've wondered precisely what I did learn from the motion picture industry that could be applied to writing. After reading dozens of scripts, and writing a few, I would guess that lessons on "writing cinematically," writing for the camera, have bled in. Working with the story material of others over a wide range of films—adventure, war, westerns, romance—became a plus. I know that all of the overseas locations and cultures now add to story settings. I benefited from observing creativity at every level. I'm grateful for having had the opportunity to be a part of film make-believe.

Done with the movie business, I was now self-employed full time at home. Not having to think of how to deal with producers, directors, and movie stars was such a pleasure, such a consuming joy, that I couldn't wait to sit down to work at the typewriter each day.

Writing doesn't consume nearly the amount of energy as digging ditches, but after hitting the keys, say, from 9:00 A.M. to 4:30 P.M., my usual day, I'm burned out, mentally and physically. A good day is eight pages, of which maybe four are keepers. Every writer I know has his or her schedule and page count, all different.

I begin a novel or a short story with a sketchy idea of the "beginning." I know less about the "middle," and I do not want to know anything about the possible "ending." I just hope I know when it's time to finish.

My usual number of drafts is six, including the final draft after the editor has had her say. I'm usually comfortable with my female editors, even when dealing with totally masculine subjects. In so far as novels and short stories go, I've only had two male editors since *The Cay*. The most drafts I've ever written numbered fourteen, *The Children's War*. Although published, and a recipient of generally good reviews, I know the faults of the work.

In most cases, I spend sixty percent of the time in research, executed before beginning the story or during it. I don't feel comfortable unless I know the people and settings—smells, wildlife, soils, extremes of weather, color and texture of flora, and every other interesting aspect. Even then, I know I haven't captured nearly the totality of each scene. Once the book is in case-hardened print, too late to change, I know it doesn't reflect the whole truth.

In 1972, *The Cay* continued to fall under rather widespread attack as a racist work, but it was still selling merrily, not an unusual occurrence. I was deeply troubled by what I thought were unfair charges against it, against me. I declared I was not a racist. I debated the book with an Afro-American panel at the Los Angeles Public Library. Librarian Binnie Tate said, "Timothy would have thrown that snotty white boy overboard." To be eaten by sharks? I was appalled.

I began to hear that the book had been taken off library shelves, both school and public. There was nothing I could do except defend it.

∽◦∾

We moved away from the beach and now occupied an old Monterey Spanish dwelling with a 180-degree sea view. Catalina Island, Long Beach, and the oil rigs in the Los Angeles Channel, not an inspiring sight, were all available on a sparkling day; boats and ships passed on the horizon. The sea still called.

I had a perfect office in the back, in a separate building which had once housed a full-time maid and gardener. Up to that time, I'd worked in cubbyholes. It was a quiet neighborhood and I hoped the constant tap-tap-tap wouldn't annoy the neighbors.

I soon sold a Western script to George Seaton. He'd separated from Bill Perlberg. The Universal production starred Rock Hudson and Dean Martin. Seaton had always wanted to do a western and *Showdown*, regrettably, was his last picture. I've always felt badly that the story wasn't of better quality. My fault. He deserved a *High Noon*.

Showdown was released nationwide in the summer of 1973 and I invited Gwen to attend the local theater with me to see my credit as writer rolling by on the big screen. A matter of ego, I readily confess. She quickly declined without stating a reason. I didn't ask for one but knew our long-torn marriage, both physically and spiritually, was at last over.

I'm reasonably sure that a part of the deep chasm that separated us was what I did for a living. A constant reminder, the tap-tap-tap of the typewriter, was probably like a drip of water from a sour stalactite. At one point, I wondered: *If the tapping stopped would she come out to see if I'd dropped dead?* Probably not. As I said before, aside from the instability of income, writers are not easy to live with. We write mentally night and day. Sometimes important family questions or statements are unheard. It is truly not much fun to be married to an obsessed writer. Only the official termination date was to be decided, lawyers to be hired. It would be cold and harsh, I knew. Rough waters ahead. More than I'd ever encountered on any ocean.

Professionally, *The Cay* had won eleven literary awards by now, despite the accusation of "racism." The one I prized the most was The Lewis Carroll Shelf Award. It deemed the book worthy of sitting on a shelf with *Alice In Wonderland*. The property was purchased by an independent team producing for Universal Pictures in late spring, 1972. The eminent black actor James Earl Jones would star, with television filming to take place off Belize. I had hopes they'd be faithful to the book since I was not given the chance to write the script, the producing team wanting to keep that money for themselves. Creators of the original work seldom approve of what comes up on the screen. On reading the script I was very disappointed. There was no scene showing the mother planting the seeds of racism in her son's mind. Why make the movie?

NBC's announcement that *The Cay* would be aired October 21, 1974, created an immediate furor in the same circles that I'd first been introduced to by the expectorating lady at the American Library Association convention.

That watchdog outfit, the Council on Interracial Books, had published a devastating review in their *Interracial Digest* in 1970 and now decided to take on NBC-TV in an effort to stop production with a phone- and letter-writing campaign to local stations, newspapers, and the network sponsor Bell Telephone. Protest calls and letters by the hundreds hit Bell.

Enlisting the aid of Dr. Samuel Etheridge, director of Civil and Human Rights for the National Education Association, the CIB persuaded Bertha Jenkinson of the Jane Addams Peace and Freedom Foundation to request return of their 1970 award, making noise in *Publisher's Weekly*. The CIB again claimed there was an "insidiously racist message" within the story.

They charged: "The black male character, no last name, conforms to the traditional stereotype of the faithful slave or retainer, happy to serve and even sacrifice his life for his 'young bahss'—a term which establishes, at the outset, the man's implied inferiority. Timothy's servility and ignorance juxtaposed with the white boy's gentility, self-assurance and erudition clearly evoke the time-worn conception of blacks as immature, self-negating, unpredictable and thus, threatening 'creatures' and whites as effectual, predictable, commanding and superior beings no matter what their age!"

I couldn't believe what was being written and publicized about this gentle story of love and understanding—my steadfast opinion.

At Rockefeller Plaza the night of the telecast, Council members carried signs of protest. It was now clear that the CIB intended to drive down retail sales and would help *The Cay* join the lengthening list of books banned from school and public library shelves.

At home in Laguna, I took the dogs for a walk at the end of the second act and have never seen the full production—nor do I have a video of it. At the time of contract signature, there were no such things as videos and I have refused to allow Universal the right to make them. There was no scene between the mother and the boy in which she poisoned him against blacks.

As usual, the telecast drove sales upward and while the picketing was noticed in the New York press, particularly the Times, I doubt that it had immediate effect on further removing the book from shelves. Yet I remained alarmed and disheartened. As a Southerner who had witnessed Ku Klux Klan action so long ago, I was all the more sensitive to the charges aimed at me personally or at *The Cay*. I was still convinced it was not a racist book. Doubleday had a different take: The CIB folks were rabble-rousers, using *The Cay* to gain attention to the Council.

Meanwhile, both Doubleday and Avon, publishers of the paperback editions, were delighted with all the controversy.

In early February 1975, ALA sent me a damning "position" paper from the Council which was going to appear in the April issue of their widely circulated, highly respected quarterly. Librarians throughout the country and overseas read it. ALA invited comment. I certainly obliged.

To The Editor:
Top of The News, American Library Association

Recently, I had the unusual experience of bundling up the 1970 Jane Addams Children's Book Award for my novel, *The Cay*, and returning it to the Jane Addams Peace and Freedom Foundation. The committee had decided, so many years later, to publicly state that the prestigious award had been a "mistake." Presented this fact, I had little desire to see it on my office wall day after day.

Charges of "racism" have been largely supported by the "under-lining" of various passages in the book, usually descriptive of the black character, *Timothy*; then the broader contention that the white character, the boy *Phillip*, was not changed by his experience with the 70-year-old West Indian who could not read nor write. Needless to say, passages in any book can be underlined for whatever purpose the reader chooses.

Directed primarily toward the white child (thinking that any black child did not need to be told much about prejudice), I hoped to achieve a subtle plea for better race relations and more understanding.

The characters of the prejudiced white boy and his prejudiced mother were taken from real life. I played with the boy and knew his mother. The character of Timothy was developed from West Indian sailors, primarily one man, but also a composite. I knew Timothy.

I told the story from the viewpoint of the white boy because Timothy needed no lessons from the white boy about prejudice, survival or anything else. If a black writer were to handle this same story, or a variation of it, I'm inclined to think that he or she would tell it from the black point-of-view, simply because of that experience. Being white, I told it from the white boy's point-of-view.

Space does not permit me to deal individually with each underlined passage that I have read in various criticisms but those most used to support the "racist" charge usually include my first description of Timothy, as seen by the racially programmed boy: *He was ugly. His nose was flat and his face was broad; his head a mass of wiry gray hair.* I realize why these words explode on paper for some people.

To be blunt, had I made Timothy beautiful, when Phillip

awakened on that raft, I could see no valid reason for marked reaction or for the hateful fires of prejudice to be refueled. Given the same story circumstance, that of conflict and transformation, I would do it again.

If a character cannot truthfully state a visual reaction to another character, one level of conflict is eliminated. If a white writer must view every black as "beautiful, wise, young and the same as every white," there can be no conflict; therefore no understanding which might possibly come out of conflict. If the black writer must say that every white is "beautiful, wise, young and the same as blacks," why bother with the story; why strive for truth?

I have been faulted for the use of dialect by Timothy, even though most West Indian sailors of 1942 spoke dialect. To me, Creole-calypso is the single most pleasing, most musical dialect on earth.

Much has also been said about my purposely "blinding" Phillip. Why could he not learn his lessons while sighted? I honestly felt that Phillip was already blind, as was his mother, long before he suffered the injury. Finally, I wanted him to reach the point where "color" made no difference, leading to the line, "Are you still black, Timothy?"

I am taking for granted that we are all talking specifically about "racism" charges against a specific book and not the uneasy issue of a writer being allowed expression on any subject, to any audience. I would hope that in any work of fiction *any* black writer could describe a white person as "ugly," as "dumb," as "different," as "racist" or anything else; choose to do what he or she wanted with the white character—girl, boy, woman or man—without fear of reprisal or intimidation from anyone.

I would also hope that the day never comes when any council, association, book award committee, political group, or government agency, can dictate to a writer; or can punish the writer, directly or indirectly, for words committed to paper.

Meanwhile, as I informed the Jane Addams committee, "I will continue to write stories as I see and feel them. I do hope that some small good will be in each one. I will also try very hard, as I have tried in the past, not to harm any human, no matter color . . . "

(Abbreviated)

I clearly remember almost falling down the steps of the two-story "Maid's and Gardener's" office house in my haste to return, *postage collect,* the Jane Addams Peace and Freedom Foundation Award. It was the four years between bestowal and taketh-away that really bothered me, the clear fact that such a supposedly upstanding organization would succumb to outside pressures.

Aside from school boards on local levels throughout the country which have been forced into hearings for the banning of *The Cay,* groups that have attempted to remove the book from school and library shelves include the National Association for the Advancement of Colored People and the African-American Parents Coalition. Over the last thirty-three years, there have been thirty-two known cases of attempts at censorship. The last known case occurred in Minnesota in 1997.

But I balance all that with the many good things that have come from *The Cay.* Long ago I was attending an International Reading Association convention in Anaheim, California, and Betty Kalagian, from the Braille Institute in Los Angeles, waylaid me in a hallway to say, "Do you know what you did?"

I thought, "Oh, my Lord, what now?" At the time, *The Cay* was still under severe attack. What else have I done? I answered, warily, "I'm sorry I don't."

Betty said, "You created the first blind child hero."

Again, I was speechless. I'd never thought of Phillip in that way. But, yes, he did live alone, without sight, and survive, on that tiny cay in the Caribbean for several months after the aforementioned Timothy died.

She said, "Blind children all over the world, reading Braille, can look up to Phillip and take comfort. The book tells them they, too, can survive something like this."

Not once did I think about blind children reading *The Cay* in Braille while I was writing it. The blinding of Phillip was an effort to make him colorblind in his relations with old Timothy. That's all. There was no other purpose.

The blindness came quite accidentally. The end result was definitely the best thing that has ever happened to me as a writer.

∽о∾

Sometimes a story idea will entrap you, beguile you, sucker you, though you know it may be a financial lost cause because the subject is of little appeal. Yet you must do it.

In the mid-seventies, I read a feature story in the *Fresno Bee* about a Basque shepherd who sang to his sheep. I was intrigued with the notion, having been told that sheep and lemmings were the two dumbest creatures on earth. Did they respond? I had a mental picture of this man sitting on a Sierras grassy knoll singing to two thousand wool-coated animals, biblical staff, his *makila*, at his side.

I wrote Louis Irigaray a letter, sending it via the *Bee*, and did not receive an answer for four or five months, thinking that perhaps he was at a sheep camp singing away, drinking red wine and eating lamb chops, completely out of touch with civilization.

Finally, a letter written by his girlfriend arrived saying that Louis Irigaray was no longer serenading his sheep. He was now singing to humans at the Bakersfield State Fair and would talk to me at that site if I so desired.

I attended the Bakersfield Fair and listened to Irigaray, who was in his mid-thirties but looked twenty-five. To my surprise, he could really sing. He was no longer performing *a cappella* to sheep. He sang both country and Basque tunes accompanied by a rather good Blue Grass guitarist. So began much fun.

As he came off the stage, good looking with coal-colored curly hair, a lady killer, I introduced myself and told him that I *might* be interested in doing a book about him. He smiled and said, "Well, I've got to think about that." I went back to his motel with him and we talked some more over several glasses of red wine.

Louie sang and sang at the Chateau Basque that night, the early evening devoted mostly to American country western but as the evening grew along, and red wine flowed, the songs were more and more Basque and the dancing was wilder, almost gypsy in pace. Men danced with men, women with women, Basque style.

Suddenly, out of the crowd of dancers came a shepherd at least six-five, his cheeks naturally red, but now a deeper red with drink. He grabbed my hands and literally threw me out on the dance floor. At his total mercy, I tried to keep his big feet from smashing mine. Once, on a twirl, I saw Louie roaring with laughter, pounding the table. *A writer must offer his body for the sake of the book.*

I was flung back into my chair when the piece ended, and Louie shoved a new glass of wine in my direction and, still laughing, said, "I'll do the book with you." That was very Basque, negative one minute, positive the next. Much laughter. We were sometimes drunk together. A writer must go with the wine.

He told me stories about the herder life. In the old days "love wagons," vehicles with clean sheeted mattresses behind the driver's seat, would go out to the sheep camps of California and Nevada. There's be a fresh rose in a glass tube by the mattress. A hooker and a sex-starved herder would have a "good time" while the driver kept an eye on the sheep and the dogs. Louie had a raft of sheep camp stories.

He took me to grazing ground in the San Joaquin Valley where one or another incidents took place, perhaps a stampede from storm lightning, coyote attacks, barley stubble fields on fire. I listened to the wild geese and heard the sand-hill cranes flying above us.

Under the stars, we could hear the wild geese coming from miles away, far out in the distance. Often, the cranes followed this same route down the valley. The sound of the night travelers would get louder and louder; then we could see their silhouettes against the velvet sky, hear their wing-beats in the deep silence. Oh, the romance of it. Oh, the poetry of it all.

Louie took me to various sheep camps that smelled of old cheese, onions, garlic, mutton jerky; lamb chops and beans and potatoes with garlic cloves; sourdough baked in Dutch ovens. There were salads of wild watercress, scooped from fast streams nearby, laced with oil and vinegar.

The dogs, the *txakurrak,* oh, the good dogs; pacing with the bands, eyes crackling with intensity, darting when an animal strayed from the path to eat, spotting any jamming and dashing to unplug it. They circled, persuading as the sheep milled, driving them back into the main flow with a bark or aggressive move. They leapt to a high place, a boulder, to observe the band. Sometimes they leapt to the backs of the sheep. I was wishing my eyes were cameras. I could have spent days just watching the *txakurrak.* Louie always sang of *"Blue," you good dog, you.* "The earth shook the day he died." I was totally enchanted with these days of research.

Writing sometimes can be much fun. Reviewers talked about the charm of *A Shepherd Watches, A Shepherd Sings* and its characters and how it revealed much about the Basque culture but only librarians and a few Basques bought it. Louie bought all the remainders and sold them at his concerts. I hope that someday a new Stephen Sondheim will do a musical about the Basques.

Doubleday took the financial hit. Most books don't pay back their costs.

⌘

There are areas, times and places and relationships that I will not write about. I do not know of any man, or woman, who does not have these shadows. Those secrets will go with me into the last sigh.

But there are truthful events that I have to address. Though as unpleasant as trepanning, they've helped me become a better, more understanding person.

The news that I was soon to be divorced came roundabout, like a curve ball, expected but unexpected, hitting the batter. Not long before Christmas, 1976, I found out about it through a family member. Why wasn't I told face-to-face by my ex-to-be? Well, the holiday season approached and my ex-to-be had decided we'd have a nice final family Yule as normal as possible. The divorce was justified but I felt defeat, relief, anger and sadness, the usual, all at the same time.

I decided to play-act through "Deck the Halls" but Christmas dawned strangely. A New Year's Eve party, with friends, at the Monterey Spanish house went on as planned, divorce unannounced, of course, but there was no last dance as the clock struck twelve. Bizarre, on both our parts.

The lawyers took over our lives in about six weeks and the immediate bone of contention, of course, were the published works, California being a community property state. Writing having possibly been a contributing factor to the downfall of matrimonial vows, it was fitting and proper that the books would play a major role in the settlement.

What little amusement I obtained from the whole mutually sorry mess came from the arguments of the her-and-his attorneys over the value of the books, present and future. Were they worth $50,000 or $250,000 or $500,000 or more? Suppose one sold for a film at $1,000,000? I kept at phone distance saying, truthfully, that I had no idea what they were worth; in frustration, I said, "Two thousand!"

Dividing assets and parental rights are usually the two most galling and painful aspects of any divorce, but the latter was no problem. Mark was at sea most of the time and Wendy, having finished Colorado State, was working for Exxon by the Golden Gate.

Michael was a sophomore in high school and would stay with his mother.

In legalese I became the "respondent" for the next weeks, months, and eventually more than two years as the lawyers (I fired my first one for being a too cheerful marshmallow) went back and forth over the dollars involved in titles dating back to *The Magnificent Mitscher,* out of print by that time.

The official post-notification weeks, the weeks after the usual Superior Court papers were served, began both uncertainly and unhappily. But then came brilliant sun and warmth one early morning on the beach.

Seven years earlier, Michael, at age ten, had appropriated a mixed-breed pup from a friend's litter, claiming it as a "Gift of God," swearing it had followed him home. The pup had been weaned two weeks previously and wasn't capable of walking the thousand yards to our house on its own. "It's okay," said the friend, dismissing the theft charge. Michael named the pup Burney. I could never figure out the spelling but let well enough alone. Burney proved to be a *you good dog, you.* I eventually claimed ownership, through default, of both Burney and Brandy Golden Boy. I wanted them badly, divorce or not.

Burney was doing his usual figure eights that morning, snapping at sand flies, when along came a widow and her huge, black mixed-breed named Oso, "bear" in Spanish. I've come to think that Burney understood my terrible post-divorce state of mind. Without any provocation at all, outweighed by forty pounds, he attacked the thick-furred brute and I yanked him away, likely saving his own hide. Later on, Oso chased us both to the top of a high rock.

I'd known of Flora Schoenleber, of Scotch-English descent, a widow who lived in the general neighborhood, for quite a while. I'd first met her at the home of mutual friends, an arranged date attended by a sprightly ninety-year-old lady who was the model for the character of "Auntie Myrt" in *Walking Up a Rainbow.* Auntie Myrt suggested that night that Flora and I begin living together, having known us all of an hour. That was premature, I thought. Lovely, and my age, Flora had glistening white hair and a quick laugh. Life in a small town tends to be a panorama of houses, names, and faces unmet, especially to dog-walkers. I knew Flora had lost her husband less than two years before; I'd seen her on the beach a number of times, wise Burney never once growling at the bear dog. Flora was a library clerk at a local elementary school, essentially "the librarian."

In the late afternoon I called her at home to apologize for Burney's behavior and inquired whether or not he'd caused any damage. I was certain he hadn't—Oso's coat was a two-inch mat— but spur of moment I decided to ask for a date.

My own vehicle was a disreputable truck so I borrowed a film editor's car and took Flora out to dinner and then to Sly Stallone's *Rocky I*, which had the appropriate theme and music for me at the time of the dueling lawyers. The courtship with my ex-to-be had been less than four weeks; the courtship with Flora was four years. We were older, wiser. She knew more about children's books than I did. We found it easy to talk. Her three children, Patricia, Michael, and Charlie, approved of me; mine approved of her.

As if court papers weren't problems enough, beloved Brandy Golden Boy, he of the female-chasing exploits, was diagnosed with leukemia. I remember one night when Flora and I took him to an animal hospital for a transfusion. Strapped on the table, he received blood from a beautiful German Shepherd lady strapped two feet away from him. I used the scene in *Tuck Triumphant*, 1991.

Brandy died one dawn in my arms on the bricks below my office/bedroom, another moment of gushing tears. Mark was home from sea and we had Golden Boy cremated, then Burney and I sadly distributed his ashes along the wintry beach at his favorite leg-lifting spots.

A few years later, Burney passed away while I was on a research trip at Hatteras and I had to walk the sands alone, tossing his ashes from the small wooden box, my heart aching. For a while, I had no four-legged partner, then Guide Dogs for the Blind called to ask if I was interested in a "career change" dog. The lady said that Hyra, in training to serve the sightless, had failed her final test. She was a golden lab eight months old. "Absolutely," is what I said and got into my truck for the five-hundred-mile drive to San Rafael, where the school is located.

As the tormented divorce days, weeks, and months went by, I tried to write, started several novels and threw away the pages. I fell back on short stories and threw away those pages. I got a contract from Random House, with a nice advance, for a book on solar energy. I worked on it for more than a year. Random properly rejected it and requested a return of half the advance. I'd done a bad job.

One day in the spring of 1979 I received a call from my ex-to-be saying that Michael had left home and what did I intend to do about it. He'd gone to San Francisco, she thought. Wendy was up there, still employed by Exxon.

He was seventeen, the very age I'd left home but for entirely different reasons. I hadn't seen too much of him since the legal proceedings had begun. He'd been working nights as a busboy at a local spaghetti joint where all the waiters were gay, occasionally dropping by the house I'd bought to begin a new life. He'd seemed okay, under the circumstances.

I called Wendy to ask if she'd seen Michael and other questions such as where was he living and what was he doing and did she know why he'd left home? From the moment she'd answered the phone, her voice had an evasive tone. Finally, she blurted, "Daddy, Michael is gay."

I must have been speechless for a moment. I refused to believe what she'd said. Michael had often been theatrical and I'd often thought his career path might go in that direction. He'd shown acting talent as far back as grade school.

I'd known fear at sea, now I knew it on land. What she'd said was impossible! There'd been nothing to indicate his being gay, so far as I could remember. I wouldn't have picked up on the signs, anyway; refusing to even consider such a devastating condition. At seventeen, did he really know? Was this a cruel device to punish both his mother and myself? I hoped it was.

Although Laguna was said to be about thirty percent gay, and had been for years, I knew practically nothing about that existence. Had it happened at the spaghetti joint with the gay waiters? I was so ignorant about homosexuals.

I was totally straight and could look back on the merry sport of girl chasing since childhood. The one and only experience I'd had with homosexuality occurred in a bar in Baltimore just before the Annibal sailed. A guy made a pass at me and I ignored him. But the sailor sitting next to me saw it and whispered, "Get out of here, I'll take care of this . . . " I got out.

I thought I'd tried to be a good dad when I was home. Camping together, Cub Scouts, I encouraged athletics and tried to be supportive in whatever he wanted to do. A motor bike? Of course. I took him on trips, including one to Point Hope, Alaska, across from Siberia, on a Disney survey. Flying bush planes, we'd had an exciting father-son time. Knowing nothing about homosexuality, I concluded it was all my fault, away from home a lot, neglect.

I flew to San Francisco and met Michael in Wendy's apartment on a foggy morning. She was at work. The deep disappointment of the meeting is still seared in my memory. *He was gay.* Clinging to hope, I said I'd pay for a psychiatrist. I'd pay for anything to say it wasn't so. I could not physically take him home in irons. I knew what my mother would have said. "He's your son. Think with your heart, not your head."

In the film business I'd met but had never really known a gay person. Now, I knew one intimately. Or did I? How most parents handle the opening of the closet door is likely to depend on how much love is there. I loved Michael very much but I did not handle what was happening very well. I wanted to stay in touch with him and used my truck to help move all his belongings to an address on infamous Castro Street, gay territory. Helping him move was a mistake but he had friends who would do it. I wanted another chance to talk to him.

He'd found work as a waiter, lying about his age, and I took Burney north, thinking that seeing his dog might influence him to return to Laguna. I was desperate. Fear again! Fear, at the age of seventeen, that he'd die up there in a city awash with drugs. That he'd become addicted. With Wendy, we met where he worked—to no avail.

I tried to write and the wastebasket filled with angry balls of paper. To cope helplessly with Michael, to fight the worry and try to sleep at night, I finally closed him off in my mind. He crept back in from time to time. I finally decided he was gay because of a strong-minded mother and a distant father, one who was away for months making movies.

Wendy was soon transferred to the international division of Exxon in New Jersey and Michael was without a family member nearby. Conversations with my ex-wife were useless. But Wendy managed to keep in touch with Michael.

Before she'd left the city he'd bought a huge motorcycle and roared up and down the city's seven hills. He was deep into drugs and began dealing. Later, a death threat from another dealer sent him fleeing to Phoenix.

I was living a novel but had no desire to write it.

While the divorce lawyers wrangled over support issues for Gwen, especially the book incomes, the relations with Michael were fragile and I was unhappily down to ghosting to earn a living. I tried to do fiction off and on during that period but seldom went beyond a dozen or so pages.

Eventually, I ghosted eight books, most of them for Random House. I was on a hair trigger during that period. I remember a shouting match with a California doctor who called me ignorant because I didn't know what hemoglobin was. His wife rushed out of their kitchen to save the day and the book.

I remember writing an autobiography for Jerry Lewis who was

performing in Las Vegas at the time. After finishing his last show about midnight he'd dine and schmooze with buddies until about one-thirty, then awaken me to talk. After three or four of those calls I phoned his agent and told him that if it happened once again I'd quit the book and keep all of the advance money. Mr. Lewis decided to talk to me afternoons.

The silliest point came when Random House assigned me to do a fitness book with Tony Caccioti, actress Valerie Harper's boyfriend. He spun me around on his shoulders in an office at MGM. I thought he'd lost his mind but finished the book. Money was the reason.

Then Michael called me from New York, a welcome surprise. His doctor had told him that he wouldn't live a year unless he quit his drug habit. By then, according to Wendy, he'd experimented "with every drug on earth." He needed to go to a drug rehab treatment center at White Mountain, Pennsylvania, a tough, army-like environment for three months. He didn't have the money. My mother would have been so pleased, Michael seeking help.

I learned White Mountain was unique in that they had post-rehab arrangements, sending their patients to Washington, D.C. where a monitor would find them jobs and check them weekly. He gave me an address and I sent the check. He's been drug-free for more than twenty years and we've become best friends.

He's a partner in a computer programming company in Ft. Lauderdale and making good money. He spends quite a bit of it on foreign travel which might date back to overseas film meanderings as a child.

LIVING VICARIOUSLY

Alcohol and smokes were my way of life while the lawyers continued to jockey around the value of the books. Vodka and papaya juice, if available, an awful mixture that made bartenders grimace, and Kools, a terrible brand of tobacco, eased me into sometimes sleepless nights. I'd awaken hoping for some kind of good news to arrive. Literary agent Gloria Loomis held my hand, looking for work.

Random House signed me to do a book on solar energy, of all things—my own idea. I went to Colorado to research the subject and then struggled to make the paragraphs exciting by exposé. I found out that the oil companies' public relations departments were scoffing at solar energy in the media, hoping to discourage possible business interest and competition.

I soon discovered that the oil companies would gladly sue Random if the book went to press. Random's lawyers—lawyers again—said no thanks. Return of half the advance money was requested. I couldn't go much lower after a year's work.

I remember those dark days were considerably brightened when letters or calls came from Mark or Wendy. I began living vicariously, mentally joining them on adventures, even thinking about using them in future books or short stories as I'd done with Wendy Lynn Appleton of the Cape Hatteras trilogy.

Wendy's solo pedicab ride on Chungking North Road in Taiwan so long ago during *The Sand Pebbles* filming, her obvious zest for adventure as a child, had not diminished.

In her senior year at Colorado State, an anthropology professor asked for volunteers to spend four summer months at Ute Mountain Ute Reservation, stark and desolate in Four Corners of four states. Wendy joined sixteen other students in a tent base at the far reaches of the tribal land eating beans, fry bread, rabbit, and goat. The latrine was built on a berm topped with tumbleweed. Wendy was assigned to teach the Ute women better nutrition. Some were breast-feeding and the babies were dying. Summer bikini beach days in Laguna were far away for this particular young lady in T-shirt, boots and shorts. I couldn't wait for the calls and letters.

She took part in a Ute sweat house ceremony and in a pow-wow and tasted peyote and listened to the stories of the elders. She donned a hard hat to help the Utes fight a devastating forest fire, hearing the roar of blazing trees as they "topped out."

She had the thrill of riding a chopper making water drops. I wouldn't have done that for all the peyote in the world. My pulse quickened. I was so glad to be her father.

૭૦૦૭

I'd like to think that I had some small influence on Mark in starting a long sea career. I took him on sports fishing boats before he was twelve, then applauded him for becoming a deckhand at age sixteen. He served aboard long-range boats off lower Mexico going for yellowfin tuna, albacore, and huge black sea bass. I was envious.

In his early twenties he became master of these boats. I once took a ten-day trip with him. Ahead of us were the dream islands of the Revillagigedo group: Roca Partida, Socorro, and San Benedicto. Fish were leaping in the Mexican tropic waters.

I sat on the bridge of the *Red Rooster* with him in the early mornings, talking man to man at last. Most of the passenger fishermen were twice as old as he was, many of them wealthy. If one was injured Mark had the training for emergency treatment before calling in a helicopter. He faced heart attacks and fish hooks caught in cheeks or eye sockets on every voyage. That took a Cool-Hand Luke to handle, I knew.

I remember Mark talking about a night when the eighty-five foot Red Rooster was drift fishing for tuna and everyone was asleep except a lookout. A submarine surfaced about a hundred years away, like the Loch Ness monster. Awakened, Mark switched on the searchlight and there it was, gray and dripping. The sub quickly motored off into the darkness. American? Russian? Chinese?

For years I followed Mark vicariously across the globe as he became mate and master of various ships that were searching for oil with satellite guidance or re-supplying oil rigs offshore. He reported side adventures such as hunting for metallic nodules on the floor of the Clarion Trench in the South Pacific Ocean. I couldn't wait for his letters about the oil surveys in the Bering Sea, the west and south coasts of South Africa, the Arabian Sea and Persian Gulf, as captain of the motor vessel *Interocean Sniffer*. Scientists were aboard to sample for oil streaks and survey the bottoms. I remember him writing about a monsoon in the Arabian Gulf that created enough wind velocity to strip his supply vessel *Cay* of all exterior paint as it ploughed into wild seas head-on.

I would have served as his mess boy for free.

Exxon had shifted Wendy from San Francisco to New Jersey where their international headquarters are located. Her mission was to sell a new computer in the Mid and Far East, actually a word processor that was the size of a Volkswagen bug. Exxon, loaded with petro-dollars, had bought up twenty-odd companies, one of which had built the "computer."

I met her in New York. We went to "The Best Little Whorehouse in Texas" on Broadway, had terrific meals and good conversations. Then she flew off to begin a new life.

In the late seventies, the part of the world that she traveled in was not set up for an American woman on her own. At the Hotel Manila, dressed her best and awaiting a prospective client in the lobby, security cross-examined her for prostitution. They studied her Exxon ID card with suspicion.

I was with her in spirit as she peddled that monstrosity called a Vydec as well as an Exxon electronic typewriter, a Qyx, and also a Qwit, an Exxon facsimile machine, all museum pieces now.

She eventually moved on to a new Exxon position in the emirate of Bahrain where her brother had once worked supplying off-shore oil rigs. Bahrain was home to the world's leading offshore banking units. The Bahrainis craved modern technology and the goodies they felt it would bring them. But they were shocked that the bearer of this technology was a twenty-five-year-old blonde from California.

One day, a prospective Pakistani client said, "I don't want your computer. I want to buy you."

Wendy sat there, open-mouthed.

The bearded, middle-aged businessman then said, "I want you to start a computer company for me." He added that the job would include a penthouse apartment, a car, a houseboy, an expense account, and, last but not least, a very good salary. He was quite willing to let her make all the decisions.

She resigned from Exxon and became an expatriate, on the go to Oman, Qatar, Abu Dhabi, Dubai, and the other emirates, as well as other Gulf nations. I was bathed in parental pride.

Month by month, week by week, I couldn't wait for further communication. She was arrested three different times in Saudi Arabia, once during the history-shattering takeover of the most holy mosque in Mecca. She got into security trouble at the Sheraton Riyadh by diving into the pool in her bikini. No woman could expose a square inch of flesh. But she was selling that mammoth machine wherever she went.

She danced and dined in the moonlit desert under tents, rugs covering the sands. She watched horse and camel races, wandered around the *souq*, the marketplace, sailed on a *dhow*, bought gold, and had tea with the king, the venerable Sheik Isa bin Kalifa.

She was living a dream life.

A Superior Court judge admonished the lawyers for playing games and decided to award half of the income of all the books written up to the time Gwen filed for divorce. Fine with me. It had been a long unhappy marriage.

A New Partner

Flora and I were married in April, 1981, after a four-year courtship. We honeymooned in the Cayman Islands. A year later, we "island hopped" around the world, beginning in Japan, with stops in Sri Lanka and the Seychelles, including a week in Bahrain to stay with Wendy.

We flew on to Munich to visit the German War Museum to research Dr. Werner Von Braun and his World War II rocket activity on Pennemunde Island, birthplace of space endeavor. The East German government refused to let me visit it personally, giving no reason. *Rocket Island,* 1984, resulted.

We ended up on the island of Sark in the English Channel to research a still unwritten novel. No autos or dogs are allowed on Sark; aircraft are not permitted to fly over it. We lived in a farmhouse and got around by donkey cart. Sark is the last haven of the feudal system.

Nineteen eighty-three produced *Sweet Friday Island,* a young adult suspense novel about a diabetic father and his daughter who were trapped on an evil island in the Sea of Cortez, off San Felipe. The question asked was, "Are any of us capable of killing another human being in defense of a loved one?" My answer is affirmative.

The fourteen-year-old daughter must make that decision to save her father's life. I'm sympathetic to diabetics, being one on a daily ration of insulin.

Mid-summer of that year I received a crushing phone call from Portsmouth: Lou Bass had died of a heart attack. He'd thought he was invincible and so had I. He'd been in the ring more than a hundred times, winning most bouts, becoming Number 6 middleweight in the world before retiring. He'd pushed his car in high heat and was finally knocked out forever.

I've never written a fight story but the memories of the crowds roaring as Lou jabbed and danced and ducked and connected will remain with me forever. I can see him now, cool as ice cubes, stalking an opponent around heavenly ropes.

A while later, I went to Broadway, experiencing another kind of joy—the world of music. Random House wanted me to do a biography. I got into my old truck and drove the sixty miles from Laguna to Beverly Hills and handed the yellow machine over to hotel parking attendants who looked upon it as if it were a four-wheeled skunk. I entered the lobby and used the in-house phone to call my prospective client. He gave me his suite number and I went up.

The smiling little man in shirt sleeves at the door was Jule Styne, the Broadway and Hollywood composer, supplying the music for such long-running hits as *Gentlemen Prefer Blondes, Gypsy,* and *Funny Girl.* His movie music included "It's Magic," "Three Coins in a Fountain," "Let it Snow." Some of his most famous show tunes included "Diamonds Are a Girl's Best Friends;" the sad, haunting "The Party's Over;" and the Streisand hit, "People"—all tunes that are played today and will be played for a long time, despite rock and rap. He'd even won the Academy Award for best song with "Three Coins" in 1954.

He invited me in and the first words I said to him were, "Mr. Styne, a terrible mistake has been made. I know nothing about music . . ."

He interrupted me. "That's why you're here. New York writers, most of them smart-asses, would be telling me what to say. I told Random not to give me a New York writer."

Though barely over five feet tall, he was a musical giant, having written more than a thousand songs. Born in London, his name had been "Jules Stein" but he'd changed it to Jule Styne, first name pronounced "Joolie." In his youth, Jule had played piano in Chicago night clubs. He'd played in gangster Al Capone's 225 Club.

For the next four months, I commuted to New York to meet with him, have breakfast at the Plaza, talk with him, tape him. He opened the doors to Broadway musicals for me. Not having an alma mater, I award myself a degree after each new book. I have a treasured unprinted bachelor's degree in Broadway Musicals, adding to Basque culture, etc.

He introduced me to musical stage greats of the time: Betty Comden and Adolph Green, Robert Merrill, Arthur Laurents, Bob Fosse, Josh Logan, Anita Loos, Ethel Merman, Jerome Robbins, Stephen Sondheim, and others. I interviewed each one and went backstage with Jule at the Winter Garden, the Shubert, and the Ziegfield.

The only problem I had with him was his use of verbal shorthand. He spoke a language all his own—*Stynese*. It defied all known syntax. Words spewed out, sentences beginning mid-phrase and left dangling, subjects changing without pause, *non sequiturs* compounded. At full throttle, his vocal chords lagged far behind his thoughts. Four ideas might be discussed at once:

Theater Dynamics: "What we in the theater call 'dynamics' is— well—fast ... but not—you can't do that—a slower tempo would— together—that's not how, well, if it's two—not right away—let's go have a cup of coffee."

I'd sometimes take a half hour to attempt to decode two or three sentences on tape, playing them over and over. He would use the machine-gun delivery during pre-staging meetings to get his way, those sitting at the table unable to understand one thing he'd said. Our last meeting in New York took place on a rainy morning. I was waiting outside his walk-up office on West 56th Street when the cab pulled up. He asked me what I knew "about mud." I told him I knew nothing about mud. He was a disastrous horse player and the ponies were running that day over in Jersey. He had a big portfolio under his arm.

After he'd fixed coffee for us, he told me he'd just completed a score for a new musical and asked if I'd like to hear some of it. "Very much," I said.

He sat down at the little red office grand piano, saying, "I sketched in a few lyrics. They're bad but they'll give you an idea." Oh, the absolute joys of research.

He began to play and noticed I had tears in my eyes. It was the timing and the mood, hearing his music in such a special concert, just the two of us, the rain coming down outside, his cigarette-scarred voice. I'm sure he planned to play a few songs but my wet cheeks got to him and he played the whole tentative score. It was for *Treasure Island,* never produced. Too expensive—not enough "angels," the monied backers.

But the whole experience with Jule Styne, who was honored by President Clinton before he died, was one of extreme joy for me. "Hayseed" Taylor of cotton-mill Statesville, N.C., backstage at the Shubert.

With the Iraq-Iran war underway, Mid-East airlines carrying Uzi-toting guards, Wendy decided to exit Bahrain after seven years and return home. She went to work for Swiss Venture Capital in San Francisco, pushing their investment services. One prospective client was Patrick Carroll, employed by Mitsubishi to buy and ship San Joaquin Valley crops to Japan. He invited her to dinner and the following year they married. Motherhood was next, the Mid-East a warm memory.

In time, Mark fell in love with school teacher Rebecca Bolen and gave up ship's bridges for a life ashore and fatherhood. An executive with the Port of San Diego, he hasn't strayed too far from the docks and commercial shipping.

THE BIG CATS

I remember with particular fondness another phone call from Gloria Loomis. "Do you know Tippi Hedren?"

I knew of her: Hitchcock's *The Birds*; Hitchcock's *Marnie*.

"Simon and Schuster wants an autobiography. You'll split the money and receive credit. Here's her phone number. Go out and see if you two can get along together." Togetherness on a non-fiction book project is always *the* most important factor.

Tippi Hedren lives on 180 acres northeast of Los Angeles, near the cowpoke town of Acton, on the edge of the desert. Palmdale, Lancaster, and Edwards Air Force Base are east of her Shambala Preserve, home to about ninety big cats the morning Flora and I drove through the sixteen-foot-high steel chain link gate. There was a warning sign on it, in English and Spanish: DANGER CLOSE THE GATE BEHIND YOU. One or more tigers could possibly escape.

As we slowly wound down a dirt road in Soledad Canyon toward her cottage, lions began to roar in No. 1 Compound and the great, guttural noise was picked up in No. 2 Compound. I stopped the truck just to listen. Soon, the roaring extended almost the full length of the preserve. Perhaps this always happened when a visitor visited. I learned it didn't. We were just lucky. I was already smiling. From what I could see, the preserve had a feeling of the *veldt*.

Tippi's home was on the banks of the usually timid Santa Clara River, a stream that wouldn't qualify as a North Carolina creek. A compound was built into the side of the cottage so that her animals could jump through her open kitchen window. One tigress would leap through and go sit down on the couch in the den, her front paws on the floor, her haunches mashing the cushions, to watch horses. Tippi would stick a western video into the VCR and off they'd go. Eventually, we watched it happen.

Tippi is a small woman, about five feet, but she has the heart and courage of her big cats.

We talked for a while about the proposed book. It would be largely taped and I would come as often as possible during the next year. Very religious, Tippi was involved in several Christian organizations devoted to feeding starving children overseas, notably Food for the Hungry. I'd fit my schedule to hers. Yes, we could work together on *The Cats of Shambala*.

Conference over, she said, "Now I'd like you to meet some of my friends."

I looked at Flora and she looked at me. We'd heard and seen her "friends" while driving by two or three compounds. We weren't ready to meet her friends. They'd been gathered for a motion picture titled *Roar,* shot on the premises, starring Hedren, her husband, her three stepsons, and her daughter, actress Melanie Griffith. The film, with some of the best big cat footage ever to pass by a lens, had opened and closed. It had fallen apart in her husband's terrible writing, usually the cause of cinema downfall. In their divorce settlement, Tippi had inherited the cats. The lions, tigers, jaguars, cheetahs, cougars, and black panthers, which are leopards, owned HER. Obsession was evident.

We followed Tippi out to No. 3 Compound where Scarface, a 500-pound lion, and Boomer, a 400-pound lioness, were watching ducks take off and land on the tiny lake near the bottom shore of their residence. We stayed close to Tippi because we were uneasy about going into this den. Uneasy is a lie.

We got within about five feet of Scarface and I stepped on a leaf, making a crackling noise. His huge head swung around and his soft brown eyes, seeming to be about the size of hub caps but in reality being no larger than a small sausage patty, examined us briefly and then looked beyond us to Tippi, a human that he dearly loved.

It was a year of education and I always waited with anticipation for her calls. "I'm home again." I went into tiger compounds with her. On entering Shambala, we left civilization behind, winding down into the Serengeti, with its granite and *gneiss kopje* boulders. There was genuine big cat smell down there. Their pee range is ten feet.

Many of the cats were adopted. Some owners had bought a cub pet and soon found they had 150 pounds of sharp teeth and sleek muscles and nowhere to keep the growing magnificent animal. Others were surplus at zoos or circuses.

The cats' moods were affected by blowing winds. The lions and lionesses hated the cold. The tigers loved it and swam around icy waters during the winter. The nights were always mysterious there. We'd wind through the compounds, Flora silent beside me, on the blackest of nights. No lights anywhere. Green eyes were everywhere staring at us. We were in their secret world. The year spent at Shambala in research and writing was so utterly unique that I hated to see it end. It was clearly another joy of writing.

Three years later, still reliving the times with Tippi Hedren's big cats, I decided not to waste the exotic background and the animals. During the tapings, Hedren had told me about a man who drove a white pickup truck, parking it alongside the county road and firing down on the cats. For her biography I said, "We're not going to use that incident. It'll only encourage some other redneck to do it again." Now I shifted the locale of the preserve to Orange County and renamed it, preserving all the surroundings, the compounds, the big cats. The book appeared in 1989 as *Sniper*.

I've been stealing from myself in this way for years, and I will continue to do so until the typewriter no longer goes tap-tap-tap. A student was murdered one night in the parking lot at Saddleback College, less than a half hour from where I live. I drove out there after sunset one evening and asked one of the campus policemen to show me where it had happened. He also told me what he knew about it. The murder has never been solved.

Deciding to shift the scene to the University of California at Irvine, up the road in the other direction, to avoid any legal problems, I proceeded to explore diplomatic immunity in connection with the killing. I understand the reasons behind the immunity; though mostly involved with parking violations, serious crimes have been committed for years under its escape clauses.

In this case, the killer of the student is identified as a staff member of the West German Embassy during the time prior to the unification of West and East Germany. Under diplomatic immunity, the killer returns to Hamburg (which I knew well from *The Counterfeit Traitor*). The student's father, a Marine colonel and veteran of Vietnam, decides to take justice in his own hands. He chases the killer through Hamburg and into Denmark, then into Goteburg, Sweden, then on to Karlstrand village, and finally out on the strange, harshly beautiful skerries above the Kattegat, where I'd been for a Columbia picture; at that point, the colonel puts him away. *The Stalker* became an HBO film.

I went back much earlier to boyhood and the Dismal Swamp, eight miles away from my home in Cradock, to set the scenes of *The Weirdo*, another young adult novel, a teenager who'd been scarred in a plane accident and was hiding in the hostile marshes with his recovering alcoholic artist father. I relived my own fears of that place with its summer night noises of millions of frogs and cawing birds and copperheads and water moccasins and elusive black bears. It won the 1991 Edgar Alan Poe award for the YA Best Mystery Novel.

I've received a lot of fan mail from *The Trouble With Tuck*, many of the letters requesting a sequel, the writing of which is always tricky—much harder than doing an original. Over several months I kicked around ideas, wrote a few sketches, and then remembered a couple in Los Angeles who'd adopted a five-year-old Korean boy by the name of Chok-do. The orphanage outside of Seoul discouraged them from flying over to pick up the child in person. He was finally sent to California via Pan Am Airways.

At LAX International, the Korean stewardess brought him off the plane and said to the family, "You're awfully brave. Chok-do can neither hear nor speak." True story! The family was in immediate shock. The orphanage had hid his condition. The adoption papers had been signed. They were stuck. I thought: Suppose the blind dog and deaf boy bond. That's all I needed for *Tuck Triumphant*, 1991.

I'd done several Christmas short stories for magazines and it was inevitable that I'd try, sooner or later, a Yule novel or novella. *Maria*, 1992, was based on a personal experience. Set in one of my favorite valleys, the San Joaquin, the Mexican family struggles with their entry into the annual small-town Yule parade. The solution lies in their oxen and hinny.

Stealing from myself again for *The Flight of Jesse Leroy Brown*, 1998, an adult biography, I remembered the Pentagon press release I'd written in December, 1950, about the Navy's first black pilot crash-landing in North Korea and dying on the frozen mountainside. I'd always wanted to do his life story. Should an Afro-American writer have put him down on paper? The answer is positively yes, but after forty-seven years none had tried to do so.

Jesse Brown was a sharecropper's son and grew up near Hattiesburg, Mississippi, falling in love with aviation when he was six or seven years old. As a student at Ohio State he vowed to become a carrier pilot, which meant breaking into the all-white club against tremendous odds. He was told, "No nigger is ever going to sit his ass in the cockpit of a Navy fighter." Oh, how wrong they were.

Imagine being the only black cadet among six hundred whites at the Naval Air Training Station in Pensacola. Imagine being at the mess table when members of your own race refuse to serve you in the sea of white. Imagine being in the cockpit of an aircraft with a white instructor who is determined to have you tossed out of the Navy simply because of your skin color. Jesse prepared himself for the ordeal every morning by looking into a mirror and repeating, "Nigger, nigger, nigger . . . "

Should that book have been written by a white man? Absolutely! No one else had wanted to do it.

Following *Jesse Brown* was *A Sailor Returns,* 2001, a rather tender story about an old sailor, thought to be dead, reuniting with his daughter and grandson after thirty years, much of that time spent in prison for murder.

The late winter of 2001 was a time of grief. Week after week, Hyra had trouble standing up. She was thirteen years old, living longer than most dogs her size, and almost ninety pounds. Finally she could no longer rise up without help. Her eyes told me that being alive was no longer a pleasure. She had arthritis. I held her, talked to her, told her what a wonderful dog she was, how much everyone loved her, as the vet ended her life. I cried for days. I want her ashes mixed with mine, then committed to the ocean.

WRITING, ETC.

Another shift of writing gears brought out *Lord of the Kill*, the sequel to *Sniper*, and a realistic fantasy, if there is such a category, *The Boy Who Could Fly Without A Motor*, both published in 2002, along with a picture book, *Hello, Arctic*.

I always cheer when I read of a book that had been rejected more than twenty times and finally found a home in a major publishing house and goes on to become a bestseller and a hit movie. I understand that John Grisham sold *A Time To Kill*, self-published, out of his trunk before it was picked up by Doubleday. *Catcher In The Rye* was rejected more than twenty times before it found a home.

Rejection—of words or love—is always painful. It is the head and stomach punch to an earnest, striving writer. But about ninety-five percent of the time, or higher, disapproval is deserved. The John Grisham cases are few in comparison to the hundreds of thousands of hopeful wordsmiths.

In this lifelong business of writing, I'd guess I've received about three hundred rejections from either magazine or book editors, mostly during the learning period. Not one did I shrug off. I usually learned from them if they were more than standard printed slips indicating no interest whatsoever. Of course, you learn from failure, not success. Witness my first book, the Mitscher biography.

Written and signed rejection comments from an editor were always studied and if two or three from respected houses generally said the same thing, then it was back to the drawing board—revision—as many times as necessary. Even then there was no guarantee that the magazine piece or book would be published.

The reasons for rejection likely range from the readers (editors) having had a dislike for the subject, a dislike of the writer, a bad cold, or a spat with a wife, husband, boyfriend, or girlfriend—or just plain bad writing. Other reasons very much include the subject not fitting the publisher's list or little chance of the subject, fiction or nonfiction, making any money. There are probably a dozen different variations of the above. I have probably encountered, at one time or another, each reason.

On the right hand side of my office leather couch is a red steel filing cabinet—story ideas in the top drawer, rejected completed book manuscripts in the bottom drawer. Open that bottom one and stench comes out. In total, they probably represent five years of writing time.

I may scan all those rejected manuscripts again and perhaps find one that may work after more revisions than it has already had. Likely, on a winter's night in Laguna, rain coming down softly, I'll consign them to the fireplace.

Will I ever be rejected again? Of course.

Another red steel cabinet contains island research covering the Sea of Cortez, Sark and the Seychelles, and other such exotic places. Boxes of research from Chinese Triad gangs to the sands of Cape Hatteras and elsewhere are in an eight-foot-long, five-foot-high, red-painted wooden cabinet out in the garage, along with two spare typewriters and the forty-odd ribbons.

Up in a small spare bedroom are my research books—foreign editions as well as English language editions. Together they describe several hundred interesting places around the world. Also up there are seven large scrapbooks dating back to yellowing bylined *Portsmouth Star* stories of the thirties. There's personal history of sorts in them. The grandchildren and great grandchildren might enjoy looking back.

∽o∾

Lord bless the dying typewriters.

Young listeners—and even older ones—usually disbelieve me when I say I still work on a standard upright typewriter, a rugged Olympia about five decades old. I need to feel the words and make use of the old-fashioned thinking time of the two-fingered hunt-and-peck system. Writing should not be measured in minutes.

I realize computers are now introduced at the kindergarten level and my youngest grandchildren, Ashley, aged eleven, and Sean, aged nine, are quite proficient with the "mouse," but I'll have nothing to do with the "interface, daisy wheel, print dot matrix" machines.

The typewriter was first patented in England, circa 1714. Dubbed "the work of the devil" by a clergyman, it competed with the quill pen. The first commercial model was introduced in the United States in 1874 by one Philo Remington. Not until 1935, the year after I first tapped an L.C. Smith, did the electric variety come on the market. All the models have served mankind nobly in war and peace. Mark Twain was the first author to use a typewriter.

About the only mechanical skill I have is that of changing light bulbs. Yet I'm told that I could conquer computers in a few easy lessons. My advisers just don't understand I was lousy with Erector sets and Tinker Toys as a small boy.

My computerized grown children and grandchildren tell me how easy it would be to make manuscript changes—just push a button and I can convert Elaine to Lisa over the course of three hundred pages in three seconds flat. They say I could make page corrections in minutes.

Truthfully, I would fear the computer as if it were a collection of wired-up snakes— humbling me, frustrating me, causing me to think more about all the electric wizardry than the manuscript.

I have no idea how many different typewriters I've used since the 1930s, perhaps thirty or more. Newsrooms, hotel rooms around the world, movie studios, home offices, the boat deck of the USS *San Pablo* and other ships have all served as platforms for my hopeful, creative labors.

Unfortunately, to my knowledge, Olympia standard typewriters are no longer manufactured so I have two to be robbed for parts when my Main Machine becomes ill. I have that supply of forty-odd ribbons, all sealed in plastic, enough to last me to when I'll be writing St. Peter's biography on that first Philo Remington machine.

Some writers keep daily journals to record any significant thoughts or events between wake-up and lights-out, a fine idea, I suppose. I don't do that, though, preferring to cull the daily newspapers and clip out off-beat paragraphs or articles, storing them by subject in file folders.

If I can't quite decide which story road I'm going to travel, I usually spend a few days checking the file folders. Dozens are in those red cabinets. Most of the time I come up empty-headed. Then somehow the idea is suddenly there, a gift out of nowhere. At least a dozen books have been out of nowhere. The one thing I'll never do again is attempt to manufacture a novel. I've tried twice. The first time was during the "hippie" era; the second time for a newspaper syndicate. Wasted months.

I've been asked why I write for children. Quite likely, the same question was asked of Hans Christian Andersen in 1838. Quite likely, he answered, "I don't," which is also my answer. I write for the sake of telling a story and am never quite sure which age will accept it.

I'm not afraid to tackle any subject, but I do limit four-letter words to "damn" and "hell," refusing to join some children's writers in using the "f-word" to demonstrate how daring they are. How stupid they are, I say. Most children have heard every earthy word in the

English language and, according to my grandchildren, aren't the least impressed. One thing I have learned about those who question why I enjoy writing for children is that a *good* book for young persons is just as difficult to write as a *good* book for adults, or more so. Having written for both levels, I'm convinced the struggle is the same; the key word is *good*.

In the books I do write for young readers, my aim is always the same: self-reliance. I hope to provide the characters with self-confidence and offer them as models in a modern, often push-pull brutal world. From the reader letters that I receive monthly, I have a feeling that the message comes through. If a middle-grade correspondent or high school student "admires" a character, I rejoice.

I am not an intellectual and wouldn't want to be. I don't understand intellectuals, so what I write is simple and hopefully easy to understand. I'm of the Rocky Riley school of "make it simple." I try to be a "show not tell" writer—showing the "innards" of a character or the twists and turns of resulting action—and that requires invention and time to get it just right.

I'm terrible at punctuation and could never be a copy editor, one who wields a wise pencil, blue or red—as distinguished from an "acquisitions editor," a comparatively new term meaning, of course, one who acquires manuscripts rather than edits them. I prefer the time-honored and more intimate editor—one who does both jobs. Most children's editors are in that category. Allyn Johnston, Harcourt, is my best editor.

I've never sent out a piece of writing that I didn't think was worthy. Thank God there are editors who said and still say, "You're wrong."

I can't help myself. Despite the risk of rejection, I must write, and addicts always risk pain.

ICU PSYCHOSIS AND OTHER OCCURRENCES

October 2, 2001, was an ordinary California writer's workday involving pages of a new novel, a survival story set in the Greenland Straits eight hundred miles below the North Pole. The early night was also ordinary in what a driveway sign proclaims *House In The Woods*, a serene property with thirty-seven assorted trees, lots of birds and Flora's multi-colored gardens, two blocks from the beach. I'd watched *Law and Order,* and after pee-walking the new dog, Betty, at about 9 P.M., I went upstairs to bed. I was sleepy but *felt fine.* No aches or pains.

About 4 A.M. I awakened with what I first thought was acute indigestion. A hammer was pounding my chest. I'd had a frustrating "silent" heart attack in 1988; an angiogram had revealed some damage but thirteen years had passed and pills seemed to be regulating the pump. Yet there was something about this symptom that was different. Thinking I'd call my cardiologist, the eminent Dr. Joel Manchester, in the morning, I got out of bed and went downstairs, sitting on the final step, waiting for the hammer to stop. I didn't think about taking an aspirin or putting Nitroquick under my tongue.

The scary, painful pounding continued and I finally awakened Flora, asking her to call 911. But the possibility of death didn't occur to me. Two fire trucks arrived a few minutes later. I was rolled down the driveway and inserted into an ambulance. First stop, at 5:09 A.M., was the emergency room at South Coast Medical Center. The immediate judgment: My worn-out motor had finally broken down. South Coast didn't do cardiac repair and the next stop was larger Mission Hospital some ten miles east where an angiogram was performed. Pictures dictated open heart emergency surgery as soon as possible. A heart pump was installed in my right groin to keep me alive.

Meanwhile, Dr. Manchester had been notified and went about assembling a skilled surgery team at Hoag Hospital to the north in swanky Newport Beach. Hoag is known internationally for its Heart Institute, and Manchester served as head cardiologist.

En route to Newport I became comatose as the team of Dr. Aidan Raney and his assistant, Erin Timmerman, joined anesthesiologist Dr. Robert Kopel in preparing to open my chest for "salvage quintuple coronary artery bypass graft surgery" and "left ventricle remodeling." I would be on the table for four and a half hours.

I remember little of October except for weird Haldol and morphine dreams. My brain had swelled and I was about to be visited by a peculiar madness. I had been a heavy cigarette smoker and I was about to pay for every match and lighter and the burn scars on typewriter tables around the world.

Meanwhile, I would put loved ones through an emotional wringer day after day while I played the ridiculous mind games. I was a terrible patient and also played physical escape games, attempting to rip out the Intensive Care Unit (ICU) life support systems. I wouldn't have blamed my family if they'd decided to let me conk out. I visited the edges of insanity.

Dr. Raney:

The comatose patient was transferred to Hoag Memorial Hospital in a very deteriorated state. He had a history of a myocardial infarction many years ago and has multiple medical problems as described in the preoperative and postoperative diagnoses. He suffered a recent acute infarct and underwent cardiac catheterization revealing severe LV dysfunction with an ejection fraction of 20% to 25%. He has multivessel coronary disease. He had a recent myocardial infarction and underwent insertion of intra-aortic balloon pump. On transfer to Hoag Memorial Hospital, he was in a deteriorating state and required emergency intubation. He was on the intra-aortic balloon pump and different catechol drips to maintain blood pressure.

Family members began to gather, aware they might be coming for a funeral. Son Mark drove up from San Diego to be with Flora as the vigil started. He became an almost daily commuter. Flora's daughter, Patricia, flew in from Illinois to support her mother. I would have been immensely comforted had I known what was happening off-stage. Michael flew in from Ft. Lauderdale. One by one both Flora's family and mine converged on Hoag. Charlie, Flora's youngest son, came up from nearby San Clemente. Mark became the platoon sergeant.

Patricia:

I arrived about midnight. Mark was asleep sitting up on Ted's office couch. I woke him up and learned that Ted had had a close call and was not out of the woods. Ted had thrashed wildly at Mission. He wanted Mark to get him out of there. That behavior continued for weeks.

> Dr. Raney:
>
> With the patient supine on the operating table after the induction of general anesthesia, the chest and legs were prepped and draped in standard fashion. A midline sternal incision was made and the sternum was split with a sternal saw. The pericardium was opened. Sutures were placed. Heparin was administered.

February 26, 2002
Fresno, California
Wendy:

You asked for my take on last October to fill in your memory gap.

The 3rd started out marked only by its ordinariness. The children were safe at school. Patrick was in China and had called home early in the morning before he flopped into his Shanghai bed. I was at a ladies luncheon to plan our next fundraiser for the local children's hospital. Sure that all was well and ordered in my life on this fall day, I had left my cell phone in the car, glad to be away from its intrusive ring. Leaving the meeting, I picked up the phone and listened to a gratingly robotic voice tell me I had eleven messages. As I listened to them, I knew the day was far from ordinary.

Oddly enough, not one of the messages told me what was wrong. But I knew from the worried tones that something was terribly amiss somewhere. Finally, I stopped listening and headed for home. Whatever the news, I didn't want to hear it on a Fresno roadside.

As if "home" could buffer whatever was to come, I gathered courage and started methodically dialing to return the phone calls. No one could be reached. Finally, finding Scott in San Francisco, he confirmed my fear that you had suffered a heart attack and were in Mission Hospital. I found the number and dialed, surprised to be put through to your room. I was even more astonished to hear your laughter and assurances that you were going to be just fine. We had a wonderful conversation. Again, just marked by how ordinary and matter of fact it was. Agreeing to talk after your upcoming exploratory procedure, I told you I loved you. You told me you loved me and I was reassured. Then it all exploded.

Dr. Raney:

1. Saphenous vein bypass graft to the left anterior descending, diagonal, obtuse marginal, posterolateral, and acute marginal coronary arteries.

2. Dor procedure, left ventricular remodeling with left ventricular aneurysm exclusion.

Wendy:

Picking up the phone the next morning, October 4, Mark told me that you were in a downhill spiral, rapidly spinning out of control. It was hard to process the news as he said, "You should head south as soon as possible." The girls were in school and the calendar was packed with clutter, but none of it seemed important. I quickly threw a strange array of clothing into the back of the car and drove to the children's schools. As I signed them out, their faces were ashen with worry, their mouths full of questions. "Is Grandpa going to live?" asked Whitney. "I don't know," I replied.

In the midst of the monotony of California Highway 99 from Fresno to Interstate 5, Mark called to tell us that you had slipped into a coma. It was hard to drive as tears spilled down my cheeks, the girls asking for comfort and reassurance that all would be well. I truthfully couldn't give it.

Five hours later, we pulled into the parking lot at Hoag. Mark and Flora were in the waiting room attached to the Intensive Care Cardiac Unit. They had had a long and miserable day awaiting word of your operation. Doctors Manchester and Raney joined us, clad in green scrubs, expressions clinical and concerned. "He's lucky to be alive. Dr. Raney saved his life," said Manchester. I held my breath.

They recited a long alphabet soup litany of veins, arteries and procedures. The bottom line? You were a very sick man and the prognosis was guarded. At that point, Manchester took over management of your struggle to recover.

Mark and I asked to see you in the Intensive Care Recovery Room. It's not a place to see anyone you love. Flora went with us. Tubes connected you to the ceilings and walls. Monitors beeped. Lights flashed. Your legs and chest were painted a noxious yellow with the Betadine solution hospitals use to prevent infections. The smell is unmistakable and unforgettable. I stroked your hand and talked to you, told you to hold on, told you I loved you. Flora and Mark added their pleas. The plethora of machines attached to you gave the only response.

The girls wandered to the Gift Shop and found a small stuffed animal that they thought you would like. They paid for it with the money I had given them to buy their dinner. It was a yellow dog, quickly named Betty. They begged to give it to you. Not knowing whether you would make it through the night, I made a decision to let them visit you. The Filipino nurses understood and helped us break the rules. All bets seem to be off when it comes to visiting a Cardiac ICU patient. Whitney and Caitlin were shocked and tearful when they saw you. This was not the vital "hellooo, you good dog" Grandpa they knew. They kissed you and tucked Betty in the crook of your arm. There she stayed for weeks to come. Patrick cut short his trip and caught a flight home from China. Our Michael flew in from Florida.

Haldol
    Helps control psychotic thinking and abnormal behavior in acute psychosis of unknown nature, acute schizophrenia, paranoid states of manic depressive disorders; helps control aggression and agitation; used to lessen delirium in LSD flashbacks and phencyclidine intoxication.

Morphine Sulfate
    Acts primarily as a depression of certain brain functions, suppressing the perception of pain and calms the emotional response to pain.

Patricia:

You were breathing but that was about all. We all held vigil, going there two or three times a day. The doctors said you might not come 'round for ten days or so due to trauma. You had had five bypasses, some valve work and rebuilding of the heart chamber. You might have only 30% of heart function after recovery.

Wendy:

Sunday, October 7th, you opened your eyes the same day President Bush gave the order to start bombing Afghanistan. The world was a mess and in our medical naiveté, we thought your world was getting better. I brought you your reading glasses, the *Los Angeles Times* and turned on football for you. Looking back, it didn't matter to you. You had no clue. But it made me feel as if normalcy was creeping back into our lives. You were intubated, a long tube wound down into your gullet, a guarantee that your body would get its serving of oxygen. Though you were tied to the bed, you kept making an insistent scissor motion with your fingers. Your eyes would plead and your hands would play. It was awful to watch and I was never sure whether you wanted us to cut the restraints, or the breathing tube, or both. You wanted to escape that prison.

Patricia:

I quickly learned just how strong Mom is. She was frightened, of course, and did not get more than a couple hours of sleep each night for the next two months, but really was thinking clearly throughout the whole process. She had her share of lost glasses, purse, and credit card episodes. But the important issues, like talking with the doctors, finding critical information, what were the most important things to do next, she was totally on top of these. I was personally and pleasantly amazed.

Michael:

You were very agitated whenever you would awake from sleeping. You would thrash around and always try to pull your lines out. They would constantly give you sedatives to make you rest. When you were awake enough to move around you would stare up to a corner of the room and bat your hands around in that scissoring fashion. You would look at us and then the corner of the room and motion towards it. Seemed like you were trying to get us to lift you up towards the light. Sometimes I would sit beside your bed and stroke your head trying to calm you down. Sometimes I thought you'd lost your sanity.

Finally they started trying to remove the breathing tubes. After the tube came out you were only allowed to suck on small ice chips at first. So you were constantly demanding ice chips from any person who walked into your room. I sat in the chair beside your bed dropping single little slivers of chips into your mouth.

Any time your tube was out they would sedate you less so you were much more animated and much more ornery. Some of the most memorable things you did were:

A.   Demand that I roll your bed out of the hospital right now. Just unhook you from all the machines, roll you down to the elevator and drive you home.

B.   Any time a nurse would walk by your room you would tell me to push your bed out into the office area so you could get him/her. You were sure they were in on the conspiracy to keep you prisoner.

C.   You kept asking the nurses and me to lift you down to the floor so you could "sleep on the deck with the dogs."

D.   And you were constantly telling me those bizarre stories about being naked, kidnapped, taken to an island.

E.   You told one of your nurses you were in love with her . . . and asked if she would stay with you all night . . . she said maybe later. It was probably a good sign that you were starting to flirt with the nurses.

I have no idea where some of your fantasies were coming from. Some were so bizarre that they definitely had to be home grown!

Only one involved me. You said you were on a bed down in the hospital basement near the nurses quarters. They kept running around half naked. A Navy chief petty officer lived down there. He'd given you a bad time. You waited until early morning, got out of bed and mashed dirt into his eyes. You said I was there that night. I wasn't. No wonder we were all worried once you were released.

The nurses and doctors were always surprised at your stamina. I'm not sure whether the nurses there were sad to see you go or not. That's what I remember ... and all in all just know it's a good thing that you don't remember most of it.

All love, Mike

Wendy:

The first time they removed your breathing tube seemed like a major breakthrough. The nurses told you not to talk, but it didn't deter you. Incredible stories kept tumbling out of your imagination, well fed by the Haldol. All the children of the Navy had been to see you, serenading you from the bed's end. The Admiral had brought them. An ever-present two-headed lieutenant seemed to be a good guy/evil doer. At times, he would thrash you. Other times he would save your life. Indians had beaten you with enormous purple-colored lily pads. You had been protected from the scorching sun by sitting in the maw of a big, black bass. Some of the fantasies seemed to transport you back to a wonderful time as you recounted your attendance at the Admiral's party at the Officers Club, the men in dress whites, the big band, the gorgeous women and lavish platters of crabs and lobster. Others were incredibly politically incorrect.

It was one long drawn out carnival ride, as reports on your condition would jerk us up and down, back and forth. At 7:35 A.M., you'd be resting peacefully. At 2:43 P.M., they would have to give you more Haldol to calm your anxiety. Bedtime you were fine and the next morning we would hear how awful your night had been. We started out celebrating each small victory as it came. We gave that up quickly—fearing the disappointment that always seemed to follow.

Dr. Manchester Notes:
I was concerned that the underlying lung disease, heart failure, and the discomfort from his surgical chest incision would overwhelm his ability to sustain normal respiration off the dreaded mechanical ventilator and breathing tube. If he couldn't do the job, eventually a tracheotomy would have to be performed.

Patricia:

Days 10-25: You had a wild stare about you. You began thrashing around in your bed, constantly kicking your legs and arms; very angry. This went on for days it seemed. Then you began to whisper. You pleaded with Mom to get you out of there. You could not grasp that you were connected to many machines. "Just take me home for three days or one day and I will come back. Just do this one thing for me." Let's just say that when you saw her you focused on this issue. She had to leave the room frequently to come up for air. Crazy stories began. Many of the stories involved fish and you being chased or beaten by men with fish. Mom thought they originated from your long beach walk at night to meet a fisherman in Baja a couple years prior. We all had doubts that sanity would return to you.

Patricia:

Crisis envelopes animals as well as humans. Betty, the dog. She would howl when we left her at home. We began to take her with us, leave her in the car and walk her in the hospital parking lot every couple of hours. This worked for a day or so, then she began to flip out. She would not stop barking. She would constantly throw herself against the interior of the car and wildly scratch to get out. She was obviously in great anguish. Anyway, it was apparent to all, after two weeks, that Betty had an "abandonment" problem and needed to be in a more stable home for a while.

Wendy:

That damned tube came in and out of your chest too many times to keep track of. Your lungs continued to be a daily nemesis and a huge worry. There was a constant parade of specialists, nurses, therapists and we pinned our hopes on each of them. We laid in wait for your doctors many times. We were seeking reassurance that you were progressing. Rarely did we get it.

Mark:

You whispered you wanted Mike and myself to hide you between us and walk down the hall and out to the parking lot.

Wendy:

One particularly excruciating day, October 17, had begun with high hopes for Flora, Pat and myself. They were dashed in a matter of seconds. The nurse pulled us aside to tell us your heart had stopped beating. The doctors had worked frantically with a thing called "external cardiac pacemaker patches" until a temporary "transvenous pacing catheter" could be emergently inserted into your heart to keep it beating. It saved your life. They call it Code Blue—

a rather colorful but innocuous term for a life and death situation. You should be proud of me for learning all these medical words but it seemed to me we were back where we'd started after almost three weeks of tension and fear. It was grim news.

Patricia:

Doctors Raney and Manchester decided that a pacemaker and a defibulator were necessary to keep you alive. It was back to the operating table and a stunning specialist, Dr. Mahnaz Behboodikah installed the automated instruments that morning. She came to us after the procedure was over and said, "He ripped his tubes out during the process and damaged both lungs." More setbacks began.

Wendy:

A few days later, three weeks of worry and uncertainty came to a head and I lost it. You had the tube down your throat, but that didn't stop you from trying to communicate with us. When you were awake, your hands were in that constant scissoring motion. Your eyes pleaded for relief. The news on your congested lungs was not good and the doctors kept upping the potent cocktail of drugs hoping to keep the agitation at bay. You and I have had some blunt and painful talks. I've received your very clear and articulate letters about not wanting to be kept alive by artificial means. Were these artificial means? Was I breaking my promise to you? Is this what the rest of your life would be? What would you want us to do?

Running from your bedside in the ICU unit that morning, I tried to find the chapel. Hoag was a mess, under renovation, and the chapel was closed. Not knowing where to go, I finally landed in the hallway leading to the Maternity Ward, adjacent to ICU, and sat on the floor and sobbed. There was some comfort in being so close to birth and promise, as life was ebbing away and dreams were ending just down the corridor. I wondered if some feeling architect had designed the floor with that thought. I must have been a pathetic figure as countless staff and visitors stopped to ask if they could help. They couldn't.

I know that God doesn't like dealmakers, but I certainly made some that day. I wasn't ready to lose you. I'm still not sure what happened in the hall that morning, but as I prayed I felt an enormous peace and comfort spread throughout my mind, as well as my body. It was an uncanny and physical response. At the risk of sheer melodrama, it was not long after that Pat knelt down beside me to tell me you were awake and doing great. And you were.

The dreaded tube came out within the next few days and never went back in again. You still had a long way to go with countless setbacks along the way. The incredible stories and fantasies continued and made us all wonder what toll the surgeries, attacks and drugs had extracted from you. Would you ever write again? Would the Ted Taylor we knew on October 2nd be back?

After a month of stasis, events began to move quickly. Once Hoag decided you were ready to leave, they wanted you out. The situation had moved from life-and-death to one of insurance rules and regs. We needed to find a place for you to go and it was obvious that you weren't ready to go back to Catalina Street. With indelible images of nursing homes imprinted in our minds, no one wanted to send you to one. Despite a ready market of seniors in similar situations, it was extremely difficult to find a "halfway" place for you to go to get the life skills you needed. We were well aware that good rehabilitation was the key to helping you get your life back. Pulling strings we managed to get you into a highly recommended hospital in the backcountry. Manchester was shocked that they would even take you. The deal fell apart and we managed to cobble it back together by hiring a 24-hour nurse to watch your every move. I wasn't there, but I know they moved you to the rehab hospital on Halloween. Dressed in a pale green nightgown, you were decked out in a black top hat and it all seemed to work. Actually, it seemed fitting.

It's now late February of the next year and I know that for you, most of all, it's been a long and strange journey. You're in a new land, with a passport you didn't ask for and don't want. It's bumpy and unfamiliar terrain for you and for us. I truly believe that it is a miracle that you are alive. It's a miracle of medicine, of will, of faith in God. I've learned some powerful and painful lessons along the way, as I am sure you have.

Most of all, I'm just glad to have you with us.

Love, WTC

I know nothing about the brain but as days and nights went by mine seemed to be capable of both terrifying and quite tranquil scenes that were so realistic that I truly believed they were real. I remained in my own body. The strangers, the actors that came upon me, sometimes touching me, sometimes talked. The settings, except in two dreams, always involved sand. I'd guess I had a dozen or more of those narco experiences. Under normal circumstances, I'm not a dreamer.

I'd always thought of myself as being a cool, submissive person, but the battle of tubes and drips and monitor wires revealed someone far different, at war with Haldol, supposedly a calming agent. Post-recovery accounts tell me that the violent thrashing that had begun at Mission Hospital began again not too long after I emerged from the darkness of anesthesia. I can only guess that I felt trapped in a strange place at the mercy of mechanical snakes.

I'm told that on certain days I was meaner than a North Carolina cottonmouth, demanding that any visitor cut me loose from the bed restraints. Let me go home! But I'm told by Dr. Manchester that a relentless will to live probably was a factor in permitting a future life. Using my fingers as scissors was simply a manifestation of that will. The poor nurses had to put up with the madness.

What baffles me are the sources of the narcotic dreams I had day and night. The psychiatrist who visited me several times in rehab said, "Well, you're a writer." But I do not have an imagination that functions that well even when awake, capable of creating LSD scenes. In living color, I found myself accepting them.

A nice looking man in a white coat seemed to visit me most mornings on the days I was awake and could comprehend, at least partially, his questions: "What's my name? Where are you?" I was at a strange beach hotel, I said.

I'd known this man a long time and knew he was a doctor but could not remember his name. He always wore a white coat. I finally connected him with an always pleasant lady named Suzy. That seemed to bother him a little. How could I know her name and not his? Haldol and morphine.

On one occasion, I said, "You're the pilot of that big yellow butterfly that flew me from Mexico to Denver. You were wearing a Luftwaffe hat. Your wife was co-pilot. We sat abreast in the cockpit." To me, that butterfly was real and flew like any regular aircraft. *ICU psychosis.* A Jewish doctor wearing a Luftwaffe hat?

On another morning I told him he was the son of a Navy pilot who was a hero of the battle of Midway in World War II. I'd written a book about that battle. His name was Stanhope Ring, an unusual name. A next door neighbor of his was a retired admiral and he went next door to inquire about Stanhope Ring. The admiral confirmed my story. *ICU psychosis.*

I was again in that tropic pool with four black naked NFL linemen. They looked as if they were 300 pounds each. They scrubbed my head with the purple lily pad.

I was naked on a sandy road with a chanting tribe of Indians in full war dress. They were feeding a bonfire and I was scared silly that they planned to roast me alive. I've never written about Indians.

I was on that same sandy road, near pine woods, lying amongst rotting fish filets, naked again. I could smell them.

I was in a complete stranger's house. He had a gun and was threatening me with it, demanding that I teach him how to write. There were other narcotic dreams that were equally as weird. I'm told that I felt compelled to share these out-of-mind experiences with family members and anyone else who would listen. Why could I remember them and not ordinary dreams?

Eventually, I was able to identify the nice looking man in the white coat: Dr. Joel Manchester. And pretty Suzy was his office manager. I've always favored females.

In total, I spent forty-six days in hospital beds but do not remember a single instant of pain aside from the first morning at home. Late in the Hoag stay I remember a bath and seeing, for the first time, the red scar-line on my chest, throat hollow almost to belly button; later, scars on the exteriors of both legs where veins had been extracted and are now doing a round-the-clock job in the vicinity of my blood pump.

It was then February, 2002, months after the pre-dawn hammer pounds, and the granting of a new life. Ah, the miracles of modern medicine.

I have loosely counted a total of thirteen healing doctors who were involved, one way or another, surgery to respiration to radiology, in the life-and-death adventure. The nurses and orderlies are countless. To all of them, especially Dr. Manchester and chief surgeon Aidan Raney, there is no way to express my gratitude.

The ordeal that I put my families through, especially Flora, who had to sign medical "risk" papers at every turn, was exhausting, emotionally and physically. Saying thank you to her is not enough.

From childhood on, I've always believed in God, whether war, other calamities, or peace. I think He was watching over me and the medical staff of Hoag the day of Code Blue when my heart ceased to beat.

SURPRISE, SURPRISE

Other *miracles* do happen. Forty-two years after I'd written *A Test of Faith* for *Redbook*'s back-of-the-book novella, Gloria Loomis called to ask if I would like to option it to two young New York TV producers, Eve Silverman and Susan Aronson? I'd almost forgotten *The Maldonado Miracle*, the full length novel that the novella had grown into. There hadn't been any interest in the story for years except those who wanted free options, a forever situation around Hollywood and Vine. I probably laughed and did say yes.

The history behind the story was simple. I'd rented a camper to take my first wife, Wendy, and Michael down to Baja Mexico, headed for a remote beach at Capo Colnett, below Ensenada. I wanted to fish and my family was game. I strapped Michael's new mini-bike to the rear of the camper and off we went. I drove over a dried, bumpy creek bed to reach the coast and in late afternoon set up a camp on a bluff above the ocean—no humans in sight, the way I always like it, being alone.

The next morning I unhitched Michael's mini-bike from the camper and off he went, up and down the dirt bluff road. The rest of us went down to the water's edge with beach chairs and settled in for a quiet morning of fishing and reading and sunning. Now and then I'd look up at the bluff to check on Michael riding back and forth. After a while I saw a Baja boy riding tandem on the bike. I thought, "How great, Michael is sharing." Then I saw the Baja boy riding alone.

We went up for lunch in the camper and Michael said, "Do you know what's going to happen to that boy? His mother died not long ago and he's going to be smuggled to the Salinas Valley where his father is." The Baja boy could speak a little English.

I thought to myself, "Suppose the Baja boy, at age ten or eleven, with his dog, couldn't find his papa in that huge Salinas Valley." I was reminded of that valley from *A Test of Faith* and proceeded to the typewriter.

Silverman and Aronson persuaded Showtime to put up the money. They hired Salma Hayek, the stunning Mexican-Lebanese actress, to direct. The film was first shown to audiences at Robert Redford's Sundance International Film Festival, earning Hayek standing ovations. Shortly after, she was nominated by Oscar voters for best actress performance in *Frida,* which she also produced. The whole wonderful experience taught me to never give up on a story, even one almost forgotten. Both the *New York Times* and the *Los Angeles Times* gave *The Maldonado Miracle* rave reviews.

Prior to the October 2001 pre-dawn hammer slams, I'd written three other books for publication in 2002. *Hello, Arctic*, with illustrations by Margaret Chodos-Irvine, is for the first-born of my grandchildren and great grandchildren and other tots. Attempting to write the text of picture books is a nightmare and I'll never try another. The art is much more important than the words.

The Boy Who could Fly Without A Motor was my first and last fantasy. It takes a special and wondrous imagination, a la J. K. Rowling, to weave the spellbound goods. Then *Lord of the Kill*, a sequel to *Sniper*, was published for young adults.

Out of the feverish typewriter in 2002 was *The Taming of Billy*

The Kid, for Harcourt, a novel about the outlaw, my first and last western. Also emerging was *A Torrent of Blood on Beautiful St. Thomas,* about terrorism in the Caribbean. Out of the typewriter in 2004 was *Ice Drift,* also for Harcourt, the 1868 story of two Inuit brothers, ten and fourteen, attempting to survive on a gigantic floe drifting south in the Greenland Straits.

EPILOGUE

February, 2004

I begin closure of these many words with a slow walk along the beach in early morning, surf running high, almost eight feet, spilling white froth for at least a hundred yards before sloshing up on the sand. There's a storm somewhere in the Southern Hemisphere.

The tide is coming in and Flora matches my steps as we dodge wide, flat sparkling swords of the sea. In less than two hours, the beach will be almost covered by the surf, and joggers and walkers like us will have to wait until the ebb is well underway, leaving behind dampness and whatever the sea has cast up.

Just as we go down the steps at Pearl Street, a flight of brown pelicans passes overhead going north, gracefully flapping wings every few seconds, lined up single file. I've often wondered how they select the lead pelican. Does it simply assume command? I'll never know. Sooner or later, they'll go into feeding mode and dive recklessly to swallow an unsuspecting fish.

Young Western Gulls are out, underparts and heads whitish. The adults have pink feet and dark gray mantles. Some are gathered in flocks. Others are airborne, out over the surf, squealing.

A few little sandpipers are happily dashing back and forth, surf to sand, "cheeping" as their tiny black feet dance to music only they hear. I've seen them on film but no composer has ever caught their rhythms to my knowledge.

The sun is rising swiftly, beginning to light up the surf and reach down into the crevices of the rocky cliffs a hundred feet away from us. It is always a glorious time to be at the lonely beach, a time to think about the day. I know that within a half hour we'll be at a bakery in an alley off the Coast Highway for coffee, and then within another hour I'll be pecking away.

It doesn't take this thoughtful setting, the cool salt breeze blowing in off the ocean, or the peace and quiet of the shore, to tell me just how lucky I've been in this life. I've accomplished most of the things I wanted to do: become a writer, go to sea, have a family.

I've been lucky in having good and caring editors, beginning with David "Pete" Glazer, who didn't realize just how precocious he was at the age of twenty. Among those who have edited my copy, I've had a few who infuriated me with their hide-bound worshiping of rules and their eager pencils. But they have been very few.

I remember one lady editor of a historical book who asked me what the condition of the harbor tide was at the Boston Tea Party. My written reply to her was: "Madam, I do not intend to research the tide tables back to 1773. What the hell difference would the tide make once the tea went into the water?"

Between newspapers, magazines and books, probably involving more than 300 editors, they've often been creative, and they have saved my professional reputation countless times. I have fought wars with some—winning some, losing some, but remaining friendly. Most of the time they have been right, I admit.

I walk along the sands with Flora and think how lucky I am to have this woman by my side. Loving and loyal. Compassionate. Fun. Guardian of my years.

Walking along the sands at a time like this, I think of my children and their children. Will they like the book? What will they learn from it? I do hope they'll all approve: grandchildren Ashley and Sean, offspring of Mark and Becky; Whitney and Caitlin, offspring of Wendy and Patrick. Then the great grandchildren, Adam and Nathaniel, offspring of Christopher Robin and Mary. Chris Robin is Mark's son, writer of mind-boggling teenage video games that take sixty hours to play. And I was lucky enough to inherit the step-children: Patricia, Michael, and Charlie. They only know the days after their mother remarried.

Writing one's own history is eventually frightening—an entire compressed life on the chopping block.

There is a special legitimate fourth grade question that brings another pained expression to teachers' faces, "When do you think you'll die?" My stock answer: "I really don't have any way of know-ing." Having just escaped that final voyage, I hope I'll drop dead over my typewriter and leave a half-finished novel to be completed by Wendy. That is an honest hope. I dread the idea of another round of hospital beds and tubes, walkers and wheelchairs. I prefer ashes from myself and Hyra being sprinkled into the ocean from a sailboat, her Dacrons puffed out in a warm wind and running sea, a toast of Haitian rum to say good-bye.

Excelsior! Excelsior!

EXCELSIOR!
Henry Wadsworth Longfellow (1807-82)

The shades of night were falling fast
As through an Alpine village passed
A youth, who bore, 'mid snow and ice
A banner with the strange device
Excelsior!   (1841)

(Source: *The Oxford Dictionary of Quotations* - New Edition)

My family, 1913, minus me.
Left to right: Edward "Riley" Taylor, mother, baby Mary,
Naoma, Louise, and Eleanor.

BIG BEAM

CAPTAIN MOUNTAIN BEARS
TACKLE

My football hero, Uncle Hugh Beam,
who would toss me ten feet into the air, 1927.

Me, going on three, in front of the "KKK ride-by" road.

My sisters, Eleanor and Mary, 1934, in a crab boat.

David "Pete" Glazer, Sports Editor, *The Portsmouth Star*, 1934.
My teacher at age 13.

October, 1942, before going off to
war, with my sister Louise,
and my mother.

Boxer and my best friend,
Lou Bass, 1941.

Gas tanker *Sinclair/Annibal*, my ship for eighteen months.
Torpedoed by a Nazi U-boat off Cape Hatteras, N.C. 1942.
(Photo courtesy U.S. Coast Guard)

Me, after diving to the bottom of the Bikini Lagoon
to plant dynamite for the atom bomb tests, 1946.

Captain Mark Taylor, master of the Cay-W, oceanic supply ship for oil rigs.

My son, Michael.

My daughter, Wendy Taylor Carroll, and Tippi Hedren's leopard.

Writer Gary Paulsen before dog team run, Minnesota, 1961.

William Holden, Denmark, 1960.

Charlton Heston during the making of
Diamond Head for Columbia Pictures, 1962.

Frank Sinatra during the making of
a documentary for 20th Century Fox, 1967.

Filming for a TV movie in Keelung, Taiwan, 1965.

My new love and wife, Flora, 1981.

My new research partner for *The Cats of Shambala*, and nice lion, Henry.

The Cats of Shambala, Lion Scarface and Lioness Boomer, his girlfriend, 1985.

Clark Gable during the filming of *But Not for Me*, 1958.

Dogs, 1989.

Mark's son, Christopher Robin, who writes and produces seventy-hour video games.

Mark's children, Ashley and Sean, with Greek goddess Hyra.

My granddaughters, Whitney and Caitlin Carroll.

My great grandchildren, Christopher Robin's sons, Nathaniel and Adam.

On the beach with Hyra, 1995.
(Photo courtesy John S. Graves)